THE IN-DE

G000123869

1

THE UNSPOILED GREEK ISLANDS

by

Anne Merewood

Published by

**Ashford, Buchan
& Enright**
1 Church Road
Shedfield
Hampshire
SO3 2HW

Printed and bound in Great Britain by
Biddles Ltd, Guildford and King's Lynn

CONTENTS

ILLUSTRATIONS

The Candid Guides
unique
'GROC's Greek Island Hotline'

Available to readers of the guides, this service enables a respondent to receive a bang up-to-the-minute update, to supplement the extensive information contained in a particular Candid Guide.

To obtain this paraphrased computer print-out, covering the Introductory Chapters, Athens, Piraeus & Mainland Ports, as well as any named islands, up to twenty five in number, all that is necessary is to:-

Complete the form, enclosing a payment of £1.50, and send to:-

Willowbridge Publishing, Bridge House, Southwick Village,
Nr Fareham, Hants. PO17 6DZ

Note: The information will be of no use to anyone who does not possess the relevant, most up to date GROC's Candid Greek Island Guide. We are unable to dispatch the Hotline without details of the guide AND which edition. This information is on the Inside Front Cover.

Planned departure dates....................................
....
Mr/Mrs/Miss..
of...
....

I possess:		I require:
GROC's Greek Island Guides	Edition	GROC's Greek Island Hotline
to:...............................	....	....
.....:...............................	....	....
....	....	....
....	....	....
....	....	....
....	....	....

and enclose a fee of £1.50. Signature..........................
Date.................
I appreciate that the 'Hotline' may not be dispatched for up to 7-10 days from receipt of this application. Please also enclose a large SAE.

Suretravel '90

A comprehensive holiday insurance plan that 'gives cover that many other policies do not reach', to travellers anywhere in the world. In addition to the more usual cover offered, the

SURETRAVEL HOLIDAY PLAN

includes (where medically necessary):
24 hour World Wide Medical Emergency Service including, where appropriate, repatriation by air ambulance.

Additionally, personal accident, medical and emergency expenses EVEN while hiring a bicycle, scooter or car.

An example premium, in 1990, for a 10-17 day holiday in Greece is £13.50 per person.

Note: all offers & terms are subject to the Insurance Certificate Cover

For an application form please complete the cut-out below and send to:
Willowbridge Publishing, Bridge House, Southwick Village Nr Fareham, Hants. PO17 6DZ

Mr/Mrs/Miss..Age.............

of...

....

I request a **SURETRAVEL** application form

Date of commencement of holiday....................Duration..............

Signature...Date.............

INTRODUCTION

It is all too easy to spend a holiday in Greece surrounded by the very people you've been trying to avoid: your fellow countrymen. Often, islands described as 'away from it all' by the holiday brochures can prove disappointingly crowded and commercialised, with very little of the real Greece showing through 'the package'. But it is out there: islands without nightclubs, fish and chips or Diet Coke - some of them even without electricity. Isolated dream beaches, friendly people, island hospitality, and spectacular scenery, unaccompanied by spectacular crowds, really do exist, if you know where to look for them.

This guide provides accurate descriptions of such lesser known Greek islands, pointing out the disadvantages, as well as the delights, of staying in more remote areas. It includes practical information to help the traveller at every stage of the journey, and background information about local history and island traditions.

Each island has been 'graded' in respect of its appeal, and separately according to the degree of commercialisation: I can safely proclaim there is no island where the inhabitants have not at least considered the possibility of tourism, even if it is obviously not a thriving industry. I have rated them by awarding numbers: for example, remote Agathonisi, with two pensions, has been awarded number 1 for exploitation, and, with fairly good beaches and a picturesque village, number 3 for appeal.

In addition, I have listed individual features of the islands, such as facilities, beaches and accessibility, and similarly graded these with numbers, with 1 being the lowest and 5 the highest accolade. So Kithira, for example, with no public transport yet at least seven weekly ferry boat connections each week with Piraeus, receives a No 2 for facilities and a No 5 for accessibility.

ACKNOWLEDGEMENTS

Particular thanks for help in the preparation of this book must go to my husband Makis, for his translation efforts, his moped servicing and driving, and for his enthusiastic support. Also to my father, Jack Merewood, for helping to prepare the outline of the maps, and to Artemis Makrigiorgos for her historical research and translation assistance.

I would also like to thank the friends who have accompanied me on my island hopping travels, and put up with tight schedules, hot walks and irritability - these include Carol and Pierra Bond, Ruth Montgomery, Dana Muller, Colin Simpson and Jane Maloney. In addition, I must thank Geoffrey O'Connell, author of GROC's Candid Guides, for giving me the go ahead, and getting me started in the travel writing arena.

No one has been more helpful than the islanders themselves, in answering dozens of tiresome questions, sketching maps, and opening their hearts and their memories to help me in the preparation of this book.

Finally there are acknowledgements to the many travellers who implored me not to write this book, in the fear that their favourite secret spot may be discovered by invading hordes - Matt and Jenny on Tilos, Valia on Kastelorizo, John on Agathonisi, and the German family who have referred to Lipsi as 'L' for the past ten years in the fear that other people may hear about it! Despite their misgivings, all these people helped me tremendously through their own knowledge and love of a particular island. In return for such kindness, I can only hope that those people who read this book and visit the islands described, will also fall into the category of Greece-lovers, and treat these peaceful spots with the respect they deserve.

The cover picture of the sea windmills north of Chios town, Chios is produced by kind permission of GREEK ISLAND PHOTOS, Willowbridge Enterprises, Bletchley, Milton Keynes, Bucks.

PART ONE
Chapter One   Planning Your Visit

When to Go
The best time of year to visit Greece is in the 'shoulder season': during the months of May, June, September or October. In June and September, fine, warm and sunny weather can be guaranteed, whereas in May and October there is a chance of the occasional cool or rainy day, but this is not usually enough to spoil a holiday.

Average summer temperatures for the Aegean islands are: May 68°F (20°C), June 76°F (24°C), July 79°F (26°C), August 79°F (26°C), September 76°F (24°C) and October 68°F (20°C). During August, the Cyclades islands are subject to the fairly strong 'Meltemi' winds.

Peak season - to be avoided if at all possible - is the last two weeks of July, and the first two weeks of August, which is also holiday time for the Greeks. Not only is the weather stifling, but the ferries are usually unbearably overcrowded, and rooms on even the more remote islands - which are often severely limited - fill to capacity. The last two weeks of August are noticeably more peaceful than the first two.

What to Take
Besides the more obvious items of cool clothing and sun cream, a traveller to the unspoiled islands would be advised to pack: soap, towels, toilet roll, salt-water shampoo, plastic bags, envelopes; clothes pegs and string for an impromptu washing line; dark glasses, sun hat, a light sweater, a long sleeved shirt (for protection from the sun), beach shoes (for protection against sea-urchins and sharp rocks), a beach mat and reading material - English language books are extortionately priced, everywhere.

Camera film is also expensive - take all photographic needs with you. Besides insect cream, most Greek supermarkets sell a highly effective mosquito 'zapper' in which it is well worth investing. This small, flying-saucer shaped contraption is plugged in, then a flat tablet inserted which, when heated by the element, gives off a vapour that rids the room of mosquitoes within about one minute! This device has even proved effective in a tent! The tablet should be changed every night.

Despite water shortages, it is not usually worth hauling around bottled water, as it soon becomes disgustingly warm. Ferries serve cold water at the bar, and cold bottled water can be bought in most shops. Of course, if you're setting off on a hike, drinking water is a must. Stores in the Athens Plaka (the old market district) sell leather thong shoulder bags designed to carry a bottle of water - very useful indeed.

Another practical item is a pocket alarm clock for early morning ferry departures - this can also come in handy for 3am disembarkations, when you need to wake up on arrival at the relevant island.

Getting to Greece
The least expensive air fares from Britain, and the USA, to Greece are

often to Athens: charter flights to islands such as Rhodes, Crete or Corfu may take you nearer your eventual destination, but are often tied in with package holiday accommodation. Still, it is always worth looking into direct flights to major islands, which eliminate lengthy ferry hauls. When searching for the best air fare, follow the advertisements in the Evening Standard or *Time Out*, if London based; otherwise the 'cheapies' in the Sunday newspapers offer the best deals, although it pays to use common sense and to be wary when checking out a particular company. I can recommend *Byzantium Travel* at 198 Seven Sisters Road, London (tel 01 281 0091) This is my favourite bucket shop with some of the lowest fares, as well as polite and friendly service - attributes sometimes lacking in the world of cheap travel.

From the USA, *Access* travel in New York (tel 212 333 7280) are probably the cheapest.

Of course, there are other ways of getting to Greece other than by air. Rail travellers often have Greece as their final destination. However, it is not advisable to buy an Interail or Eurail pass if you intend to carry out most of your travelling in Greece, as buses, rather than trains, constitute the most widespread form of public transport and serve far more destinations. The rail route through Yugoslavia to Greece is long and tedious, and a ferry from Italy is a much more pleasant way to enter the country.

This latter point is relevant to those considering travelling to Greece by car, as driving through Yugoslavia is reputedly difficult and uninspiring (the inland stretch, at least). On the other hand the ferry is a comfortable and reasonable alternative. Compared to the price of cross-Channel fares from Britain to France, for example, the car ferry from any Italian port (Ancona and Brindisi being the two major points of departure for Greece) is incredibly good value. These boats are far superior to Greek inter-island ferries: spacious, air conditioned, clean, and with superb facilities. Most of them call in at Corfu and Igoumenitsa before terminating at the Greek port of Patras. Foot passengers can take connecting buses from Patras on to Athens, buying their tickets on the ferry. There is also a rail connection from Patras to Athens.

While it is advisable to make reservations for cars in advance, especially in July and August, passengers can almost always buy tickets on the spot.

The cheapest way to Greece from England is still by bus. It is also the least comfortable and the most exhausting. Tickets can be bought both in the UK and in Athens (try the student travel shops on Nikis Street, near Syntagma Square). The trip usually lasts four days, and passengers have the option of disembarking and rejoining the bus, *en route.*

At the opposite end of the scale is the package holiday. While the tour company giants are more often than not present on the smaller islands, some smaller companies have specialised in 'away from it all holidays', which have the advantage of combining ease and comfort with a tranquil holiday. Before opting for one of these deals, check to be sure that the destination is really as remote as they proclaim. If it's included in fifty guide books to Greece, or on the 'beat' of the major tour operators, this is unlikely. Some companies really do a good job, and one I would particularly recommend is *Twelve Islands*, of Angel Way, Romford in Essex (tel 0708 752653). They are present on virtually every island in the Dodecanese (their speciality) - even in such locations as Marathi and Kastelorizo. They prove their 'away-from-it-all' intentions by even offering 'Robinson Crusoe' holidays on uninhabited rocks: they provide a boat and all the equipment. (Make sure you like your travelling companion...).

Getting to the Islands

Travelling from the mainland to less well-known islands is not always simple. Few have airports and some are only visited by one ferry a week. As Greek ferries can occasionally prove unreliable, and are affected by weather conditions, it is all-important to allow enough time, at each end of the vacation, for travelling between the airport and your isolated beach - even if this means spending a night or two in a 'tourist hub'. Olympic Airways fly from Athens to some smaller islands, and many travellers consider a thirty minute plane journey more attractive than a twenty two hour boat trip. Internal plane fares are inexpensive compared to Britain, though considerably more costly than the ferries. However, don't arrive in Athens expecting to immediately buy an internal air ticket to a popular destination - in high season seats sell out about two weeks in advance. The option of reserving tickets from your destination island, back to Athens, when you first arrive in Greece, should be seized at once. Tickets can be purchased at Athens airport, or at the Olympic Airways offices in Syntagma Square and on Singrou Street. Islands with airports almost always have an Olympic Airways office.

Hydrofoils are another speedy alternative to ferries, taking about half the time, but charging twice the price. Unfortunately, their range of destinations is limited. Which brings us to the usual method of inter-island travel... the ferry boat.

I have only once witnessed a scheduled Greek ferry being declared full, and refusing to take on any further passengers. But more than once I have pondered the odds of survival if the ferry I was on were to sink. Considering that in July and August, the lifeboats are usually filled with passengers who can't find space to sit down, even before the boat departs, presumably they would not be very high. Still, at least this means that, conveniently, one can get off the plane and head straight for the Athens port of Piraeus, assured of a ticket... to somewhere.

Express buses run direct from the airport to Piraeus, and all Olympic Airways staff speak English, if you have any problems or questions. The easiest way to get to Piraeus from the airport is by taxi, which are the cheapest in Europe. Very occasionally a taxi driver may try to cheat a foreigner, so be sure the meter is running - if he does not, simply refuse to pay. Between midnight and 5am, the driver is within his rights to double the fare.

If you spend time in Athens, before heading to the islands, tourist information, the Olympic Airways office, and a major subway stop are all based in or around Syntagma Square. The National Tourist Office of Greece (NTOG or EOT) has a desk in the National Bank, and issues an accurate, extremely useful, weekly updated timetable of all the ferries leaving the ports of Piraeus   and Rafina. The Tourist Office have numerous other helpful handouts, and all the staff speak English.

Tickets for the boats can be purchased at the individual offices of the particular ferry boat line, or more simply at the port prior to departure. I never really understand why anyone uses the myriad ticket offices in Piraeus, as shipping officials usually establish a temporary ticket table just beside the ship, about an hour before departure. Tickets can even be purchased on board, after the ship has sailed.

From Athens, the easiest way to reach Piraeus is on the one subway line, which terminates at the port. Travel on Athenian public transport is free before 0800hrs, and very inexpensive at all other times. The practice of offering free ferry tickets to remote islands, to encourage tourism during the low season, operates some years, but has recently been discontinued. This may, or may not be a permanent state of affairs.

Getting Around the Islands

Fortunately, nearly all island destinations have their ports in logical places, since few islanders have cars, and need to ease their transport problems. In most cases, the island's major facilities for visitors are probably located in the vicinity of the ferry boat quay. Port settlements have expanded over the past century, especially during recent years when commercial reliance on the ferries has grown. Many islands, which used to produce their own crops, are now depopulated and farming has all but ground to a halt. Supplies - and money-bearing travellers - arrive on the quayside, and so the villages have edged down the mountain to meet them!

In days of yore, island planning worked the opposite way round: pirates were 'thick on the sea', and defenceless little houses spread around the harbour were sitting targets. Thus the island capital (usually known as 'The Chora', from the Greek word for town) was frequently situated away from the port, sometimes out of sight on the reverse side of a convenient mountain. This practice is to be found on most Aegean islands, including the more popular locations, though modern-day ports have often expanded so much, due to the demands of tourism, that the fact is easy to miss. The islands Ios, Siros, Milos, Siphnos and Patmos are excellent examples of this 'design'.

Travelling away from the port sometimes poses a problem, especially on islands such as Tilos and Kithira, where there is no organised public transport. However, most islands with roads have one or more buses and taxis which meet the ferry. In the absence of either, the island's transport system usually takes the shape of a pickup truck, or a communally used three-wheeler, and drivers are prone to offer lifts. On islands which are growing in popularity, but still don't have buses, pickup truck owners make a summer living out of driving tourists about, with the names of their destinations chalked on boards, above the cab.

Even the smaller islands may have car rental, but generally the best way to establish independence is to hire a scooter. Petrol can prove to be a precious commodity, with the once a month deliveries frequently delayed.

If there are no petrol stations, the only source of fuel may well be the hire firm, so think twice before heading off to far-flung destinations, without a petrol station at the end of the road!

I must warn, rather than advise, that a Greek island is not the best location on which to learn the art of motorcycle riding - especially on unspoiled islands, where the road surface is more often than not absent. Still, hundreds do it - but expect to be daunted at first by the rocky and sandy tracks you'll be travelling.

If there is no bus, no moped or bicycle hire, no taxi, and perhaps no road (which encompasses Arki, Marathi, Donoussa, Agathonisi, and Chalki, among others), it will be necessary to walk, or hitch-hike. A more devious tactic is to proclaim one's extreme interest in some inaccessible location, in the hearing of any sympathetic islander. This tactic rarely fails, and has resulted in the offer of a lift from one side of an island to a remote monastery on the other side, not only for me, but for my friend as well as her five year old, plus a week's supplies and belongings.

One last note. The fond phrase in popular guide books, "if all else fails take a donkey", is a romantic myth. Donkeys are now rarely available for hire by travellers, even in out of the way places and islanders don't sit around offering lifts to tourists - they are far too busy carrying crops or local supplies. Sikinos island is an unusual exception to this rule, and on Santorini the animals are a commercial necessity.

Accommodation

Not many unspoiled islands boast five star hotels. Many don't have hotels at all - they get by with pensions and rooms in private houses. Where hotels are present in remote areas, they are often of the old fashioned, 'Greek-provincial', style: high ceilinged, sparsely furnished, creaky, 'unhappily' plumbed, with stone or linoleum covered floors, and no light shades. On the other hand a few, isolated, super-modern hotels are appearing, some for the express use by small package holiday companies. These are usually constructed by islanders, who, after a lifetime abroad, have saved enough US or Australian dollars to return home and create a dream hotel, on the island of their birth. If an island does not have such a 'luxurious castle in the air', there will probably be talk of one being established... in the near future.

The distinction between the old and new hotel is striking: the former are very often pale ivory coloured and peeling, with ornate but rusting iron balconies, the whole place giving the impression that it could collapse, at any moment. The modern hotel, on the other hand, appears to go out of its way to sparkle, with white walls, brightly painted doors and shutters, and more often than not would look equally in place in Benidorm or Majorca!

Similarly the quality and appearance of pensions can vary, but in out-of-the-way places they are usually basic, friendly, simple, and acceptably clean.

Rooms in private houses, the least expensive accommodation, are full of character and usually very clean, especially on the islands described in this guide, where householders still take a pride and pleasure in their hospitality. The facilities may be basic, and the 'standard' rooms plainly furnished. It is not uncommon for the 'parlour' to be turned into a summer 'room for rent', and this will more likely than not still contain the family paraphernalia - portrait photographs, bureaus, glassware, and other knick-knacks. On other occasions, the entire family sleep in one room, or even outside, turning over their whole house to guests.

In hotels, pensions and rooms, accommodation may have a private, en suite bathroom, or share the facility with other guests. In A, B, or C class hotels, the bathroom will almost inevitably be en suite.

Prices vary tremendously, depending not only on the classification, but from island to island. It would be nice, but not entirely accurate, to state that obscure islands are less expensive than popular ones. True, the least expensive must be Nisiros, but, in comparison, rooms at Marathi island's only taverna (where the generator and running water are supported by tourist income) cost considerably more than budget accommodation in many popular spots. Be that as it may, as a general rule, accommodation is inexpensive and you are far less likely to be 'ripped off' on an unknown island than you are in a popular tourist centre.

Availability of accommodation is another situation which can run contrary to expectations. It must be stressed that, despite low numbers of visitors, many rarely frequented islands are barely able to cope with any number of tourists, and what little accommodation there is fills quickly, in peak season. Being first off the ferry is not a bad idea. Where the port accommodation is full, outlying villages - maybe the Chora - can more often than not offer something, and even if nothing is advertised, rooms can be tracked down by asking about.

Camping is illegal in Greece, except in designated campsites. However, if there are no rooms, the police, short of whistling up a ferry and throwing all excess tourists into it, have little choice but to turn a blind eye to beach campers. Sites are established on many of the larger, more popular islands, but are rare elsewhere. Although you are unlikely to be moved on, even if the island has available accommodation, it is best to be tactful, as camping brazenly on a beach next to unfilled rooms does little for international relations - camp discreetly, if you must!

Prices tend to increase in line with Greece's rather alarming inflation rate - around 20% a year, which is why they have not been quoted in the text. However, accommodation has been rated on a comparative scale (inexpensive, reasonable or expensive). In general, this book covers the budget, lower end of the market. Note that prices increase during high season but fall substantially when plenty of rooms are available. In theory, all pensions and private rooms should display their rates in the room, but this is not always the case. Many room owners are reluctant to let accommodation for one night only, and may ease their charges accordingly.

Food and Drink
Tavernas are widespread on the islands, because Greeks, be they Athenian businessmen or fishermen, eat out as a way of life. Generally this is only

marginally more expensive than cooking for yourself, so even budget travellers can eat extremely well. And as for the wine - it really can be almost as cheap as water!

The fare at the average, lesser known island taverna, will be well cooked, but possibly restricted in variety. This does not apply to Lefkas, where tourists are well catered for, but on Agathonisi, for example, the bread will be stale after two days, with no more available until the next supply boat arrives. On Sikinos most tavernas only serve meatballs after July 25th!

Seafood is generally pricey, but one bonus of the 'undiscovered' islands is that fish is frequently less expensive - this is particularly true of Kastelorizo and Nisiros. On the other hand, fresh fruit and vegetables, not to mention bread, can often be a real problem if the island only receives one or two supply boats a week. Where this is the case, the vegetable market may open for a few hours, after the boat docks (even if this occurs in the middle of the night), and then close again for the rest of the week. Learn the ropes, if you want your own supply of fresh fruit and snacks - find out when the next ship is due, and be sure to do all your shopping then. Travellers are often fooled by the fact that the shops are full on the day they arrive - with supplies from the ferry they've just left! But they will not remain so for long.

Between islands, most ferries offer reasonable, if sometimes greasy snacks, such as mini pizzas, doughnuts and sandwiches. A picnic makes a pleasant alternative. It is also a good idea to stock up every time you pass through a 'hub' island. For example Kos has a particularly wonderful fruit market not far from the ferry boat quay.

As for drinking... wine is probably not only cheaper, but more plentiful than water, in most places, although local shortages are taken care of by bottled water, available at most stores. Frequently a village has a communal tap (as in Livadia on Astipalia) served by fresh spring water, and island water is almost always pure enough to drink, though some well water has an earthy taste.

Retsina, resinated to preserve it in the heat, is the best known Greek wine, although there are many other non-resinated wines available. Ouzo, and Metaxa brandy, are the national spirits; German beer is widely available for the less adventurous. Alcohol is generally inexpensive, and licensing laws are non-existent. As for under-age drinking, one particular TV advertisement for nationally available Cambas wine shows an eight year old boy buying the wine in a store for his family!

Children, Women and Men

Having travelled in the company of a five year old for one month around the lesser known islands, I would advise anyone considering taking a young child to do so, with no reservations. One of the only concessions made in the past, when accompanied by a child, was to decide against spending a few days in a deserted monastery, an hour's hike from the nearest house, because there was a snake or two in evidence... In most cases, a child can prove a benefit, rather than a drawback. Greeks are famed for their love of children, and villagers prove even more friendly and helpful than usual towards travellers with families in tow. Child abuse is non-existent, and even if you lose sight of your family on the beach, someone else will be keeping an eye on them! Any child under seven years of age can be referred to as a baby, and established with a camp bed in a room for two - usually at no extra cost - in fact many room-owners won't take payment, even if the child sleeps in a 'regular' third bed.

Greece has a lot to offer children besides sea and sand. Your offspring will leave the islands loaded with sweets, starfish, drawings from other children, and the conviction that Greeks are the nicest people in the world.

The most common catastrophes are the unexpected medical ones. On a remote island there may be less chance of emergency treatment, although the islanders have to cope with these things themselves. Furthermore, a helicopter is always attainable, by courtesy of the military, if it is necessary to resort to such desperate measures. But Greece is not an unhealthy country - if local water is non-potable, the bottled variety is that which everyone else drinks too.

As for women travelling alone, Greece differs from, say, Italy and Spain, when it comes to problems with men. Especially on the less developed islands, you are very unlikely to attract any unpleasant attentions. On the more tourist visited islands, such as Kos and Corfu, *et al*, the local youth indulge in 'kamaki' - literally 'harpoon fishing', but also the term used to describe the alternative sport of picking up foreign women! Greek males in tourist resorts seem to believe all women with white (or red) skin are an easy catch, unless proved otherwise. And there the difference lies - a healthy hint of the 'otherwise', and you will find that the men retreat. The 'game' has a light-hearted nature, and although such attentions can be irritating; dangerous or threatening situations almost never arise, even in Athens, in the middle of the night. As Greeks 'live' in the streets, there are always people about and men will desist, if you ignore them.

This is even more true of the unspoiled islands, because in small communities, where tourists have had little impact, men treat women with great respect. Indeed it is often foreign women who offend the locals' sensibilities, rather than the other way round!

Communication

English is very widely spoken, and even on the farthest flung rock of all, people may surprise with their knowledge of the language. Where this is not the case, schoolchildren love to serve as interpreters, otherwise ex-merchant seamen, a product of even the most humble of Greek islands, possess some English, picked up on their travels. The other 'source' of English-speaking islanders are those who have lived overseas, usually for long periods, in America or Australia. Some islands, like Kithira and Karpathos, have a great tradition of the inhabitants emigrating, and suddenly, totally unexpectedly, it seems everyone around you understands English. In contrast, those islands with an indigenous capacity for supporting their populations over the years have experienced fewer emigrants, thus very little English is spoken. Take a phrase book, and a sense of humour. Where the island has an Olympic Airways office, the employees speak English, otherwise a likely bet is the schoolmaster, the policeman or possibly the doctor.

Older residents on an island often speak the language of a former occupying power, for example, the Dodecanese islanders speak Italian, and Lefkadians speak some French, and Italian too. The latter island was not only occupied by the Italians, during the Second World War, but the inhabitants continue to trade with Italian vessels and, more recently, Italian tourists have become established. Despite which, a little Greek goes a long way. Islanders (with the exception of certain waiters, who tend to answer in an irritating manner, with fluent English) are delighted to hear foreigners attempting their language, which so few people ever learn. A 'holiday Greek' course before leaving home definitely proves helpful in the more remote areas.

Communication with the world, outside of Greece, is often more difficult than communication with the local population. Most islands have an OTE office, for sending telegrams, and making international telephone calls. On outlying islands these offices are usually only open weekdays, between 0830-1500hrs. On some larger islands they open at the weekends as well, whilst the busiest places are open 24 hours a day, seven days a week.

If the OTE office is closed, there is sometimes a local 'everything' shop with a metered telephone. Make the call and the shopkeeper charges when finished. The large red telephones with coin slots are for local calls only. Kiosks also have phones, as do hotels, but the overall problem is usually not the availability of machinery, rather the poor quality of the line. It can take many frustrating minutes to even get a connection out of an island, let alone out of Greece. This is due to tourists overloading a system which, by most European standards, is inefficient and inadequate, even when phoning from the heart of Athens. Patience usually pays off, and you will break through the communication barrier, eventually, but don't plan to call home at a pre-arranged time, because this is overly optimistic.

Of course, these helpful hints assume that the telephone system is actually in operating order... When I was last on Kastelorizo, no-one had been able to telephone from the island for a month, although incoming calls occasionally got through - at the sound of a ringing telephone, all the villagers leapt to their feet, in wonder. Even the port police could not advise of the impending ferry boat's arrival! I have known the radio telephone on Arki to similarly be out of commission...

I read an American article about the Greek islands which blamed the lack of telephones on the fact that Greece was a socialist country. One may well quibble over the use of the word socialist... but does the writer seriously imagine there were plenty of telephones during the years of the dictatorship?

By courtesy of Geoffrey O'Connell, author of the GROC's Candid Guides'.

The Alphabet

Capitals	Lower case	Sounds like
A	α	Alpha
B	β	Veeta
Γ	γ	Ghama
Δ	δ	Dhelta
E	ε	Epsilon
Z	ζ	Zeeta
H	η	Eeta
Θ	θ	Theeta
I	ι	Yiota
K	κ	Kapa
Λ	λ	Lamtha
M	μ	Mee
N	ν	Nee
Ξ	ξ	Ksee
O	ο	Omikron
Π	π	Pee
P	ρ	Roh
Σ	σ	Sighma
T	τ	Taf
Y	υ	Eepsilon
Φ	φ	Fee
X	χ	Chi
Ψ	ψ	Psi
Ω	ω	Omegha

Groupings

αι	'e' as in let
αυ	'av/af' as in have/haff
ει/οι	'ee' as in seen
ευ	'ev/ef' as in ever/effort
ου	'oo' as in toot
γγ	'ng' as in ring
γκ	At the beginning of a word 'g' as in go
γχ	'nks' as in rinks
μπ	'b' as in beer
ντ	At the beginning of a word 'd' as in deer
	In the middle of a word 'nd' as in send
τζ	'ds' as in deeds

Useful Greek

English	Greek	Sounds like
Hello/goodbye	Γειά σου	Yia soo (informal singular said with a smile)
Good morning/day	Καλημέρα	Kalimera
Good afternoon/evening	Καλησπέρα	Kalispera (formal)
Good night	Καληνύχτα	Kalinikta
See you later	Θα σε δω αργοτερα	Tha se tho argotera
See you tomorrow	Θα σε δω αύριο	Tha se tho avrio
Yes	Ναι	Ne (accompanied by a downwards and sideways nod of the head)

No	Οχι	Ochi (accompanied by an upward movement of the head, heavenwards & with a closing of the eyes)
Please	Παρακαλώ	Parakalo
Thank you	(Σαζ) Ευχαριστώ	(sas) Efkaristo
No, thanks	Οχι ζυχαριστώ	Ochi, efkaristo
Thank you very much	Ευχαριστώ πολύ	Efkaristo poli
After which the reply may well be:-		
Thank you (& please)	Παρακαλώ	Parakalo
Do you speak English?	Μιλάτε Αγγλικά	Milahteh anglikah
How do you say....	Πως λενε...	Pos lene...
...in Greek?	...στα Ελληνικά	...sta Ellinika
What is this called?	Πως το λένε	Pos to lene
I do not understand	Δεν καταλαβαίνω	Then katahlavehno
Could you speak more slowly (slower?)	Μπορειτε να μιλάτε πιο αργά	Boreete na meelate peeo seegha (arga)
Could you write it down?	Μπορειτε να μου το γράψετε	Boreete na moo to grapsete

Numbers

One	Ενα	enna
Two	Δύο	thio
Three	Τρία	triah
Four	Τέσσερα	tessehra
Five	Πέντε	pendhe
Six	Εξι	exhee
Seven	Επτά	eptah
Eight	Οκτώ	ockto
Nine	Εννέα	ennea
Ten	Δέκα	thecca
Eleven	Εντεκα	endekha
Twelve	Δώδεκα	thodhehka
Thirteen	Δεκατρία	thehka triah
Fourteen	Δεκατέσσερα	thehka tessehra
Fifteen	Δεκαπέντε	thehka pendhe
Sixteen	Δεκαέξι	thekaexhee
Seventeen	Δεκαεπτά	thehkaeptah
Eighteen	Δεκαοκτώ	thehkaockto
Nineteen	Δεκαεννέα	thehkaennea
Twenty	Εικοσι	eeckossee
Twenty-one	Εικοσι ένα	eeckcossee enna
Twenty-two	Εικοσι δύο	eeckcossee thio
Thirty	Τριάντα	treeandah
Forty	Σαράντα	sarandah
Fifty	Πενήντα	penindah
Sixty	Εξήντα	exhindah
Seventy	Εβδομήντα	evthomeendah
Eighty	Ογδόντα	ogthondah
Ninety	Ενενήτα	eneneendah
One hundred	Εκατό	eckato
One hundred and one	Εκατόν ένα	eckaton enna
Two hundred	Διακόσια	theeakossia
One thousand	Χίλια	kheelia
Two thousand	Δύο χιλιάδες	thio kheeliathes

Lofos		Hill
Moni/Monastiri	Μοναστήρι	Monastery
Naos	Ναός	Temple
Nea/Neos	Νέο	New
Nissos/Nissi	Νήσος	Island
Odhos/Odos	Δρόμος	Street
Ormos	Όρμος	Bay
Oros	Όρος	Mountain
Palios/Palaios	Παλιός	Old
Paralia		Seashore/beach
Pediada		Plain
Pelagos		Sea
Pharos		Lighthouse
Pigi		Spring
Plateia	Πλατεία	Square
Potami	Ποτάμι	River
Prokimea		Quay
Spilia	Σπηλιά	Cave
Steno		Straight
Thalassa		Sea
Vuno	Βουνό	Mountain

Useful Greek

English	Greek	Sounds like
Where is...	Που ειναι	Poo eene...
...the Olympic Airways office	τα γραφεία της Ολυμπιακής	...ta grafia tis Olimbiakis
...the railway station	ο σιδηροδρομικός σταθμός	...sidheerothromikos stathmos
...the bus station	ο σταθμοζ των λεωφορειων	...staihmos ton leoforion
...the boat	το πλοιο	...to plio
...the nearest underground station	ο πλησιέστερος σταθμός του ηλεκτρικοο	...o pleessiestehros stathmos too eelektrikoo
...the ticket office	το εκδοτήριο των εισιτηρίων	...to eckdhoterio ton eessitirion
...the nearest travel agency	το πλησιέστερο πρακτορείο ταξιδίων	...to pleessiestehro praktorion taxidion
I'd like to reserve...	Θέλω να κρατησω	Thelo na kratiso
...seat/seats on the	θέση για	...thessee/thessis ghia
...to	για	...ghia
...plane	αεροπλανο	...aeroplano
...train	τραινο	...treno
...bus	λεωφορειο	...leoforio
...ferry-boat	πλοιο	...plio
When does it leave/arrive	Ποτε φευγει/φθανει	Poteh fehvghi/fthanee
Is there...	Υπαρχει	Eeparhee...
...from here to	απ εδωστο	...Apetho sto
...to	στον	...ston
Where do we get off	Που κατεβαινσμε	Poo katevenomhe
I want to go to	Θέλω να πάω στους ...	Thelo na pao stoos...
I want to get off at	Θελω να κατεβω στο	Thelo na katevo sto...
Will you tell me when to get off	Θα μου πείτε πού να κατέβω;	Thah moo peete poo nah kahtevo
I want to go to...	Θέλω να πάω στους ...	Thelo na pao stoos
Stop here	Σταμάτα εδώ.	Stamata etho
How much is it	Ποσο ειναι	Posso eene
How much does it cost	Πόσο κάνει η μεταφορά	Posso kani i metafora
...to	στο	...sto
Do we call at	Θα σταματήσουμε στην ...;	Tha stamatissome stin

Signs often seen affixed to posts & doors

Greek	English
ΑΦΙΞΙΣ	ARRIVAL
ΑΝΑΧΩΡΗΣΙΣ	DEPARTURE
ΣΤΑΣΙΣ	BUS STOP
ΕΙΣΟΔΟΣ	ENTRANCE
ΕΞΟΔΟΣ	EXIT
ΚΕΝΤΡΟ	CENTRE (as in town centre)
ΕΙΣΟΔΟΣ ΕΛΕΥΘΕΡΑ	FREE ADMISSION
ΑΠΑΓΟΡΕΥΕΤΑΙ Η ΕΙΣΟΔΟΣ	NO ENTRANCE
ΕΙΣΙΤΗΡΙΑ	TICKET
ΠΡΟΣ ΤΑΣ ΑΠΟΒΑΘΡΑΣ	TO THE PLATFORMS
ΤΗΛΕΦΩΝΟΝ	TELEPHONE
ΑΝΔΡΩΝ	GENTLEMEN
ΓΥΝΑΙΚΩΝ	LADIES
ΑΠΑΓΟΡΕΥΕΤΑΙ ΤΟ ΚΑΠΝΙΣΜΑ	NO SMOKING
ΤΑΜΕΙΟΝ	CASH DESK
ΤΟΥΑΛΕΤΕΣ	TOILETS
ΑΝΟΙΚΤΟΝ	OPEN
ΚΛΕΙΣΤΟΝ	CLOSED
ΩΘΗΣΑΤΕ	PUSH
ΣΥΡΑΤΕ	PULL

Useful Greek

English	Greek	Sounds like
I want...	Θελω	Thelo...
...a single room	ενα μονο δωματιο	...enna mono dhomatio
...a double room	ενα διπλο δωματιο	...enna thiplo dhomatio
...with a shower	**με ντους.**	...me doosh
We would like a room for...	Θα θελαμε ενα δωματιο για	Tha thelame ena dhomatio ghia...
two/three days/a week/ until	**δυο/τρεις μέρες/μια** εβδομαδα/μεχρι	thio/trees meres/meea evthomatha/mekhri
Can you advise of another...	Ξερετε κανενα αλλο...	Xerete kanena alo...
house with rooms	**σπίτι με δωμάτιο**	speeti meh dhomatio
pension	πανσιον	panseeon
inn	πανδοχειο	panthokheeo
hotel	**ξενοδοχείο**	ksenodhokheeo
youth hostel	**ξενώνα νέων;**	xenonas neon
How much is the room for a night?	Ποσο κανει το δωματιο για τη νυχτα	Poso kanee dho dhomatio ghia ti neektah
That is too expensive	Ειναι πολυ ακριβα	Eene polee akriva
Have you anything cheaper?	Δεν εχετε αλλο πιο φθηνο	Dhen ekhete ahlo pio ftheeno
Is there...	Υπαρχει	Eeparkhee
a shower	ενα ντουζ	doosh
a refrigerator	ενα ψυγειο	psiyeeo
Where is the shower?	Που ειναι το ντουζ	Poo eene dho doosh
I have to leave...	Πρεπει να φυγω	Prepee na feegho...
today	σημερα	simera
tomorrow	αυριο	avrio
very early	**πολυ νωρίς.**	polee noris

| Thank you for a nice time | Εὐχαριστω για την **συμπαθητική ώρα** * | Efkareesto ghia tin simpathitiki ora |

*This is the exact translation, which would never be used, however, in Greek. An expression meaning rather: 'thanks for the fun' is:

	Εὐχαριστω για την διασκεδαση	Efkaristo ghia tin thiaskethasi
Where can I hire a...	Που μπορώ να νοικιάσω ἐνα	Póo boro na neekeeaso enna...
...bicycle	ποδήλατο	...pothilato
...scooter	σκούτερ	...sckooter
...car	αυτοκίνητο	...aftokinito
I'd like a...	Θα ηθελα ἐνα	Tha eethela enna...
I'd like it for...	Θα το ήθελα για	Tha dho eethela ghia...
...a day	μία μέρα (or: μιά)	...mia mera
...days	**μέρες**	...meres
...a week	μία εβδομάδα	...mia evthomadha
How much is it by the...	Πόσο κάνει την	Poso kanee tin...
...day	μέρα	...mera
...week	εβδομάδα	...evthomadha
Does that include...	**Συμπεριλαμβάνονται σ' αυτό**	Simberilamvanonte safto
...mileage	τα χιλιόμετρα	...tah hiliometra
...full insurance	μικτή ασφάλεια	...meektee asfaleah
I want some	Θέλω	Thelo
...petrol (gas)	βενζίνης	...vehnzini
...oil	λάδι	...lathi
...water	νέρο	...nero
Fill it up	Γεμίστε το	Yemiste to
...litres of petrol (gas)	**... λίτρα βενζίνης.**	...litra vehnzinis
How far is it to...	Πόσο απέχει	Poso apechee
Which is the road for...	**Ποιος είναι ο δρόμος για ...;**	Pios eene o thromos ghia
Where are we now	Που είμαστε τώρα	Poo eemaste tora
What is the name of this place	**Πώς ονομάζεται αυτό το μέρος;**	Pos onomazete afto dho meros
Where is...	Που είναι	Poo eene...

Road Signs

ΑΛΤ	STOP
ΑΠΑΓΟΡΕΥΕΤΑΙ Η ΕΙΣΟΔΟΣ	NO ENTRY
ΑΔΙΕΞΟΔΟΣ	NO THROUGH ROAD
ΠΑΡΑΚΑΜΠΤΗΡΙΟΣ	DETOUR
ΕΛΑΤΤΩΣΑΤΕ ΤΑΧΥΤΗΤΑΝ	REDUCE SPEED
ΑΠΑΓΟΡΕΥΕΤΑΙ Η ΑΝΑΜΟΝΗ	NO WAITING
ΕΡΓΑ ΕΠΙ ΤΗΣ ΟΔΟΥ	ROAD REPAIRS
ΚΙΝΔΥΝΟΣ	BEWARE (Caution)
ΑΠΑΓΟΡΕΥΕΤΑΙ ΤΟ ΠΡΟΣΠΕΡΑΣΜΑ	NO OVERTAKING
ΑΠΑΓΟΡΕΥΕΤΑΙ Η ΣΤΑΘΜΕΥΣΙΣ	NO PARKING

Have you a table for...	Εχετε ἐνα τραπέζι για	Echete enna trapezee ghia...
I'd like...	Θέλω	Thelo...
We would like...	Θέλουμε	Thelome...
a beer	μιά μπύρα	meah beerah
a glass	ἐνα ποτήρι	ena poteeree
a carafe	μιά καράφα	meea karafa
a small bottle	ἐνα μικρό μπουκάλι	ena mikro bookalee
a large bottle	ἐνα μεγάλο	ena meghalo bookalee
bread	ψωμί	psomee
tea with milk	τσάι με γάλα	tsai me ghala
with lemon	τσάι με λεμόνι	me lemoni
Turkish coffee (Greek)	Τούρκικος καφές	Tourkikos kafes
sweet	γλυκός	ghleekos

medium	νέτριος	metreeo
bitter (no sugar)	πικρό	pikro
Black coffee	Nescafe xwpis γάλα	Nescafe horis ghala
Coffee with milk	Nescafe με γάλα	Nescafe me ghala
a glass of water	ενα ποτήρι νερό	enna poteeree nero
a napkin	μιά πετσέτα	mia petseta
an ashtray	ένα σταχτοδοχείο	enna stachdothocheeo
toothpick	μιά οδοντογλυφίδα	mea odontoglifidha
the olive oil	το ελαιόλαδο	dho eleolatho
Where is the toilet?	Που είναι η τουαλέττα	Poo eene i(ee) tooaleta?
What is this?	Τι είναι αυτό	Ti ine afto
This is...	Αυτό είναι	Afto eene
cold	κρύο	kreeo
bad	χαλασμένο	chalasmeno
stale	μπαγιάτικο	bayhiatiko
undercooked	άψητο	apseeto
overcooked	παραβρασμένο	paravrasmeno
The bill please	Το λογαριασμό παρακαλώ	To loghariasmo parakalo
How much is that?	Πόσο κάνει αυτό	Poso kanee afto?
That was an excellent meal	Περίφημο γέυμα	Pereefimo yevma
We shall come again	Θα ξανάρθουμε	Tha xanarthoume
Where is...	Που είναι	Poo eenne...
Where is the nearest...	Που είναι η πλησιέστερη	Poo eenne i pleesiesteri
baker	ο φούρναρης/ψωμας	foornaris/psomas
bakery	Αρτοποιείον	artopieeoń
bank	η τράπεζα	i(ee) trapeza
bookshop	το βιβλιοπωλείο	to vivleeopolieo
butchers shop	το χασάπικο	dho hasapiko
chemist shop	το φαρμακείο	to farmakio
dairy shop	το γαλακτοπωλείο	galaktopolieon
doctor	ο γιατρός	o yiahtros
grocer	το μπακάλης	o bakalis
hospital	το νοσοκομείο	to nosokomio
laundry	το πλυντήριο	to plintirio, (plintireeo, since i = ee
liquor store	το ποτοπωλείο	to potopolio (potopoleeo)
photographic shop	το φωτογραφείο	to fotoghrafeeo
post office	το ταχυδρομείο	to tahkithromio
shoe repairer	το τσαγκαράδικο	to tsangkaradiko
tailor	ο ραπτης	o raptis
Have you any...	Εχετε	Ekheteh...
Do you sell...	Πουλάτε	Poulate...
How much is this...	Πόσο κάνει αυτό	Posso kanee afto...
I want...	Θέλω	Thelo...
half kilo/a kilo	μισό κιλό/ένα κιλό	miso kilo/ena kilo
aspirin	η ασπιρίνη	aspirini
apple(s)	το μήλο/μήλα	meelo/meela
banana(s)	η μπανάνα/μπανάνες	banana/bananes
bread	το ψωμί	psomee
butter	το βούτυρο	vutiro
cheese	το τυρί	tiree
cigarettes (filter tip)	το τσιγάρο (με φίλτρο)	to tsigharo (me filtro)
coffee	καφές	cafes
cotton wool	το βαμβακι	to vambaki
crackers	τα κρακεράκια	krackerakia
crisps	τσιπς	tsseeps
cucumbers	το αγγούρι	anguree

disinfectant	το απολυμαντικό	to apolimantiko
guide book	ο τουριστικός οδηγός	o touristikos odhigos
ham	το ζαμπόν	zambon
ice-cream	το παγωτό	paghoto
lemons	το λεμόνια	lemonia
·lettuce	το μαρούλι	to marooli
map	το χάρτης	o khartis
a box of matches	ενα κουτί σπίρτα	ena kuti spirta
milk	το γάλα	to ghala
pate	πατέ	pate
(ball point) pen	το μπικ	to bik
pencil	το μολύβι	to molivi
pepper	το πιπέρι	to piperi
(safety) pins	μια παραμάνα	mia (meea) paramana
potatoes	οι πατάτες	patates
salad	η σαλάτα	i salatah
salami	το σαλάμι	salahmi
sausages	το λουκάνικα	lukahniko
soap	το σαπούνι	to sapooni
spaghetti	σπαγγέτο	spayehto
string	ο σπαγκος	o spangos
sugar	η ζάχαρη	i zakhahree
tea	το τσάι	to tsai
tomatoes	η ντομάτες	domahdes
toothbrush	η οδοντόβουρτσα	odhondovourtsa
toothpaste	η οδοντόκρεμα	odhondokrema
writing paper	το χαρτι γραψίματος	to kharti grapsimatos

English   **Greek**
Stamps   ΓΡΑΜΜΑΤΟΣΗΜΑ
Parcels   ΔΕΜΑΤΑ

Map nomenclature	Greek	Translation
Agios/Ag/Ayios/Aghios	Αγιος/´Αγια	Saint
Akra/Akrotiri	Ακρωτήρι	Cape/headland
Amoudia		Beach
Ano	Ανω	Upper
Archeologikos (horos)	Αρχαιολογικός χώρος	Ancient (site)
Cherssonissos		Peninsula
Chora/Horo/Horio/khorio	Χωριό	Village
Kato	Κάτω	Lower
Kiladi		Valley
Klimaka		Scale
Kolpos	Κόλπος	Gulf
Leoforos	Λεωφόρος	Avenue
Limni	Λίμνη	Lake/marsh
Limani	Λιμάνι	Harbour

PART TWO
The Cyclades

The Cyclades are the quintessential Greek islands. Here are the 'typical' Greek scenes - shining white capitals 'icing' arid brown mountains, glistening cobalt blue domes capping white churches, deep turquoise seas lapping against white beaches and sheer red cliffs. The Cyclades have it all - including the largest share of the tourist trade.

Santorini, Mikonos, Paros, Naxos - they're all in this area of the Aegean, seething with people. But - you guessed it - there are a few islands which still hold on to their Cycladean beauty, and yet manage to escape from the brunt of the tourists. Read on...

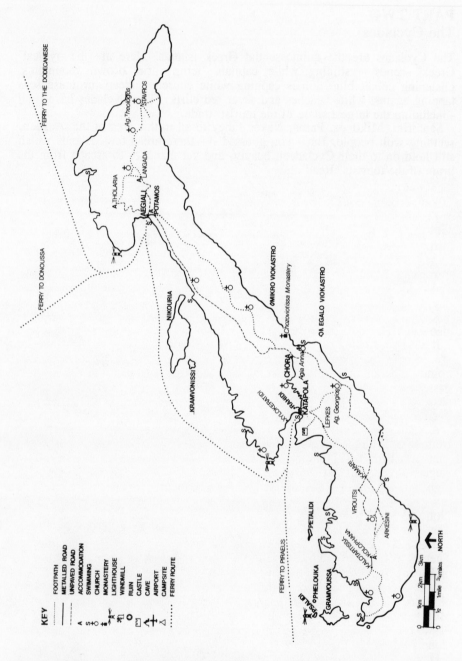

Illustration 1 Amorgos island

CHAPTER TWO   AMORGOS

On a Scale of 1 To 5:	Sites to visit: 4
Appeal: 3	Accessibility: 5
Exploitation: 3	
Beaches: 2	Population: 1,500
Scenic beauty: 4	Telephone prefix: 0285
Accommodation - standard: 2	Size: Around 29km, at its
Accommodation - availability: 4	longest, and 10km across, at the
Facilities: 4	broadest point.

Location
The most easterly island in the Cyclades, Amorgos lies approximately 30km south-east of Naxos island and 40km north-east of Santorini.

Getting There
Airport: No.

Ferries: Many ships call at Amorgos, on their way to the Dodecanese, making for a frequent service, which averages out at about one boat per day, in high season.
Katapola, in the south-west, is the island's main port but nearly all ferries also call at Aegiali, the northern port, a further 45 minutes by sea.
It is worth finding out, in advance, where the ferry is coming from if you are heading back to Athens. For some boats, Amorgos is a turn-round point; others arrive 'hot' from the Dodecanese, loaded down with passengers, and have been known to dock and depart so hurriedly that few passengers have been able to disembark, let alone enter the highly overcrowded ship.
A small, local ferry (presently the FB Skopelitis) is based at Katapola, from where it connects some four times a week with Naxos, as well as the islets of Koufonisi, Shinoussa, and Iraklia. It travels twice a week to Aegiali(Amorgos) and Donoussa, and also makes one weekly venture, in high season, as far as Ios and Santorini.

General
The island is long, narrow, and massively rocky, with spectacular cliffs and a dramatic coastline. It has poor beaches, pretty villages and bad roads. There was little communication, in the past, between the island's two ports of Katapola and Aegiali - nearly all ferries still stop at both - and the best way to travel between them remains by sea. Amorgos has some grand and glorious sights: rocky mountains and sea views, the Chozoviotissa Monastery, bright flowery streets, and picture postcard mountain villages, of which Langada is the most stunningly beautiful. For these highlights alone, it is worth a visit.
Having said that, Amorgos is not ideal from other points of view. It has a

few quirks which are distinct from its essential character and yet have an influence on the visitor. Accommodation tends to be overpriced in Katapola, much of it being low quality, and the beaches to the south especially, are uninspiring. In addition, the island seems to attract more than its fair share of drop-outs - giving Aegiali, in particular, a whiff of Amsterdam in the sixties, rather than Greece in the nineties. Aegiali's campsite is their focal point, which location sees its fair share of illegal substances, thus posing an increasing threat to the previously crime-free island population. A few of Aegiali's bars play deafening music, to cater for an atypical clientele - atypical, that is, on an 'unspoiled' Greek island.

Despite, or perhaps because of this, the numbers of tourists are not over-powering, and the 'unusual' atmosphere disappears outside peak season.

Because there is little overlap between the two ports, or the two ends of the island, I have chosen to treat them separately.

Katapola

The main port is composed of three small settlements which almost run into each other: Katapola 'proper' centred around the ferry quay, **Rachidi** in the middle of the bay, at the bottom of the road to the Chora, and **Xylokeratidi**, opposite the ferry quay, across the bay.

Accommodation

Plentiful, and room owners meet the boats, even in high season, but as mentioned before, Katapola's rooms are overpriced. There seems to be a pact among the owners to charge the same for their accommodation, whatever the quality, and this price is at the top end of the 'reasonable' scale, even if the state of the room is not. An unclean double room with a shared, almost outdoor shower and toilet, is as expensive as a clean, en suite bedroom. Dirty rooms (as opposed to those with the occasional dusty specks) are rare on the islands, but I have experienced quite a few here, especially in the Xylokeratidi district. The area behind the ferry boat quay may prove a better bet, added to which there are a couple of small hotels.

Rooms in the Chora are quieter and less expensive.

Camping This port has one basic site with stony ground and limited shade, set in the fields between the settlements of Rachidi and Xylokeratidi. There is a small taverna and washroom, as well as clothes washing facilities. The site is D category - but it looks 'D-luxe' when compared with the 'below-basic' site at Aegiali, though both charge the same rates. Some 'away from it all' campers prefer Agia Anna beach, which has the rare luxury of a water tap (see Beaches).

Food and Drink

There are plenty of tavernas in the area of the ferry quay - my favourite is Diogenes, at the extreme end of the bay. The Akroyiali, on the square, opens up for the 0500hrs ferry and serves breakfasts, as well as main meals. There are also a few tavernas in Xylokeratidi, but I recommend readers to avoid Gabalos, which I found to be dirty, as were its rooms!

A pleasant alternative to the busy tavernas in Katapola can be found in the Chora, where a couple of cafes serve food at lunchtime and in the evenings. I liked the Cafe Loza.

Vital Information

There are no banks in Katapola - the general store near the quay, and the man at the ferry ticket office, just below the seafront square, carry out money transactions, but both prefer notes to traveller's cheques. Eurocheques can be changed at the post office, but this is up in the Chora, and very well supplied it is too, with airmail letters, *poste restante*, postcards and maps. The Chora has a bank, but it doesn't engage in exchange.

Transport to the Chora is surprisingly convenient - the Amorgots received a godsend two years ago, in the shape of three buses for Katapola, and one for Aegiali, which they utilize to the utmost! There are hourly connections to the Chora, and daily links to the outlying villages in the south-west (see Excursions). Note that the Katapola bus does not connect with Aegiali but, in high season, a van from Aegiali makes the trip to the Chora, twice a day, mornings and evenings.

There is a hard-to-find taxi, and two businesses offer moped hire, which is superfluous as the bus service more than adequately covers the area, added to which the roads are badly surfaced.

Still, if you rent a moped and fall off, a doctor is handy - in the administrative block on the seafront, at the junction with the road to the Chora. This building also has an advertisement for rooms, above the clinic. The dentist is further up the road, in the middle of Rachidi. Near the ferry quay is a pharmacy, situated on the left of the narrow street which leads away from the right of the 'kiosk square' (sea behind one). The shop is just beyond the port police, who are on the right of the same street.

Other shops concentrated around the Katapola area include a couple of general stores, a bakery, on the seafront, fruit and vegetable stalls, a kiosk, in the square, and a few trendy souvenir shops.

There is no OTE office, though a couple of the general stores have metered telephones. The OTE is in the Chora, beside the square on which the port bus parks - it is open until 1500hrs, weekdays only.

Beaches

The Katapola beaches are not great, in either quantity or quality. Around the bottom of the bay is a narrow strip of grey sand with pebbles, but the sea at this end of the inlet is uninvitingly brackish. If you wish to swim, the best bet is to walk right around and out on the footpath beyond Xylokeratidi, and the village cemetery, to a series of small coves with not-very-good beaches, but cleaner water. There are a few similar coves exactly opposite across the bay, but they are even smaller.

Basically not a good place to swim, the nearest alternative is:

Agia Anna Beach The bus leaves the port every hour for this beach, calling at the Chora *en route*. As indicated, the islanders have embraced wheeled transport with enthusiasm - it is quite amazing that, considering the low numbers of tourists present, their bus service is so wonderful (compare it, for example, with the dreadful public transport on the more developed island of Kithira). Even more surprising is that, after leaving the Chora, the bus ventures down a steep mountainside to get to the beach! The dirt road drops down the cliff face in a series of terrifying hairpin bends, with which the bus usually copes, though on occasions the driver has to back up when he misses the turn. Added excitement comes from the fact that there can be up to ninety people on board at any one time (I have counted!). One young driver, in particular, enjoys herding people in, crying, "We can all fit in, if we want!". No surly officiousness here! A chance meeting with a pig and her litter may add to the memorability of the experience.

The beach is worth the ride, if only because there isn't any alternative within striking distance! In its favour, it is marvellously situated at the bottom of a 180 metre cliff, with grand views up to the distant monastery, and across the sea to the island of Astipalia. The water is brilliantly clear, and the cliff and boulders provide some shade. On the other hand, after a ten minute scramble around the rocks (which are piled against the bottom of the cliff, as though a landslide occurred only five minutes ago), the large pebble beach is usually rather crowded, since it caters for all the tourists in the area. It is definitely a nudist beach, but is at a reasonable distance from habitations, after all.

One big advantage is that fresh water is piped down from a spring in the rock face, making the beach a good place to camp. Those who prefer not to scramble or 'nude' can stick to the flat rocks near the chapel of Agia Anna, close by the bus turn-round.

Sites to See

The Chora From a distance, the island capital is less striking than many other Cycladean Choras, lying as it does across the saddle of the hill, rather than clinging to the top of a mountain. The town is dominated by the remains of a Venetian castle, built by the Ghizzi family in the 13th century, on top of and around a massive lump of rock.

Despite first impressions, the Chora's streets are as lovely as the 'best of them', being spotlessly whitewashed and in a good state of repair. And hidden away are a few, very pretty, small squares with tasteful cafes and some discreet bars, as well as indigenous kafenions, pokey general stores and public buildings.

The Chora has rooms, and makes a pleasant, inexpensive alternative to staying in Katapola.

Chozoviotissa Monastery Every island has its monasteries, but few, if any, are like this one. Chozoviotissa is one of the Amorgos high spots, and should not be passed by in any circumstances.

As highlighted in the Agia Anna description, amazingly the bus from Katapola, via the Chora, visits the monastery every hour throughout the summer. It used to be a tough trek down the rocky road from the Chora, but now is a tough ride - less taxing on the body, but perhaps more taxing on the nerves! Incidentally, be sure to take the bus marked Agia Anna beach. The daily bus to Kato Meria does not go to the monastery, whatever the driver says! The correct bus spills out monastery passengers at the end of a rocky path, half-way down the cliff towards the beach. From here it is a ten minute, uphill walk to the church. As with all Greek monasteries, shorts and bare shoulders are prohibited. Women should wear knee-length skirts. The building looks like one giant white buttress, supporting a massive cliff-face, which overhangs it at a disconcerting angle. Viewed side-on, it is broad and flat - seen from outside the front entrance, it is a slender sliver of white against the rock. Chozoviotissa is open to the public, mornings and evenings and, surprisingly, the few monks still in residence, carry on the tradition of offering all visitors coffee, water and Turkish delight when they end their short tour of the chapel and balcony. This courtesy must be a hangover from the days when only a few hardy souls hiked out here every week - now, making refreshments is a full-time job for one of the six monks.

The monastery was constructed during the early 9th century AD, destroyed by pirates, and rebuilt in 1088. There are two stories as to how it came into being, both involving the inevitable icon. One, in keeping with legends concerning most Greek island monasteries, claims that the icon arrived, on its own, in a boat. On this occasion having been set afloat by a woman who was afraid of the iconoclasts in the Palestinian town of Chozova, hence the monastery's name. A somewhat more plausible explanation is that the icon was brought to Amorgos by Palestine monks, also expelled by iconoclasts, but from the Chozeva monastery, which was set on a towering cliff, just like the one on Amorgos. Tradition also claims that during their journey, the monks were attacked by pirates off Cyprus, and the icon smashed to bits. As the monks were trying to glue the picture back together, it became miraculously complete, with no traces of the damage remaining.

Other classic stories abound. One was that the workmen were originally constructing the monastery a kilometre away but every day found their tools moved to the present-day site. They eventually gave in and built it there instead. Up until 1952, a spear was inexplicably embedded in the cliff-face, high above the monastery tower - legend claims that it marked the exact spot where the monastery was to be built. It eventually fell down ('by the will of God'), and is now stored in the chapel.

The Virgin is accredited with many miracles on Amorgos, not least of which is her personal protection of the monks from the rocks that constantly fall on the roof from the cliff overhang! However, she missed one in 1976, which crashed through three floors, but repairs have since been carried out.

This monastery was one of the wealthiest in Greece, until the state removed much of the church's property, in 1952 - the same year in which the spear fell out of the rock - surely an omen after all?!

Minoa The remains of ancient Minoa, on the mountain above Kapsali, are worth a short visit, and the route up to Minoa makes a lovely evening hike. From the back of Katapola port, take the stepped path, which sets out on the left, behind the blue and white church, and can be clearly seen wending its way upwards above the town. The steeply climbing track joins a rough road and, near the summit, a signposted path to the right is marked Minoa.

The walk along the ridge affords excellent views of the coast, and the Chora is also visible above Katapola. Minoa lies beyond a wooden gate, where the sign proclaims, 'Excavations of the Greek Archaeological Society, 1981'.

The remains are apparently of an acropolis, a gymnasium and a temple to Apollo - a mixture of huge hewn stones, and smaller walls which look like the foundations of ordinary houses. The torso of a broken statue stands mute amid the ruins.

Excursions

Kato Meria A bus leaves Katapola every morning (twice on Sundays) for all the villages in the south of the island - collectively called Kato Meria ('Lower Places'). For those who are intent on getting away from it all, or who want to walk and explore the southern part of the island, this could be an ideal base for three or four days. There are rooms at **Kolofana**, and plenty of hikes in the area, some of which I describe.

The best map for walkers is a large black and white map drawn by a German, Dr George Perreiter, and available in various tourist shops. This shows contours, as well as many sites of interest, in detail, and is produced in English.

Even as a one-day excursion, the trip is worth making - it takes one and a half hours to reach the final destination, then the bus waits for three hours, near the small beach of **Ormos Paradision**, before making the return journey. Sit on the left side of the bus for the best views.

Stopping first at the Chora, the bus continues towards Agia Anna Beach, but turns right at the junction. Here follows the most spectacular part of the drive, along the top of the cliffs, with splendid vistas.

After a while, the road passes the small monastery of **Agios Giorgos Balsamitis** (down a short track to the right). This religious house, surrounded by a patch of fertile land, is currently inhabited by just one monk, and has a view down the valley to Katapola. (Incidentally you can reach this monastery on foot from Katapola, taking a left fork in the track to Minoa - the monastery path is painted white in places, and the church is visible above you.) The story of how the monastery was founded is typical of many island churches. A shepherd grazing his flock noticed that one of his goats regularly disappeared, every day. He followed, only to find a spring with fresh green grass. To his surprise the grass seemed to grow back immediately it was cropped, so he concluded that this must be a holy place. These suspicions were confirmed in a dream, during which St George instructed him to dig at the site of the spring. This he did, turning up, surprise, surprise, the holy icon of St George.

The story of magical goings on since the monastery was founded, however, are even more unusual. Until quite recently, water from the spring, 'Laloussa', was believed to have mysterious powers and was collected in a vessel to be 'read' by the monks to predict the future. Islanders used to visit the monastery for consultations on all things - marriages, journeys, business deals. This activity was banned by the church, about fifty years ago, as being unholy.

Beyond the monastery, the first village reached is **Kamari**, lying in a shallow valley between two gently rising hills. The bus stops at a small cafe, delivering bread as well as the passengers.

This general area is also referred to as 'Vroutsi'. From here, a path leads back in a north-easterly direction to the hamlet of Lefkes, and then on to Katapola, joining the mountain path down from Minoa. This is a pleasant walk, taking from three to four hours. Between **Lefkes** and Katapola the road is passable by moped, but between Lefkes and Kamari, only on foot.

Two beaches on the south, and one on the north coast are accessible from Kamari, but all are difficult paths. The German map is the best source of information in this regard.

The bus's next stop is a bread delivery to the Taverna O Makis, in **Arkesini**, where the low-lying, white cube-like buildings are thrown into relief by a magnificent, painted church. Arkesini is near the site of an ancient city, Kastro, of which only scant remains are now visible. The best preserved ruin is that of a fortress, with a square tower surrounded by a courtyard, and located a few minutes' walk to the north of the village, at the area called **Agia Trias**. If you intend to spend time in Arkesini, there is a path down to a beach on the south shore, but it is a steep, stiff climb. To get there, walk back along the road about 1km towards Kamari, then follow a path to the right, which descends to the deserted, shingle beach of **Amudi**.

The road continues across wheat fields, and agricultural plains, punctuated by smooth, paved threshing floors. These shining circles - many still in use today - were, they say, the dancing floors of countryside nymphs, on whose help and goodwill the farming community depended at harvest time. To attract these naiads, farmers placed a clean white towel, filled with grapes and figs, and a jug of water in the middle of the field.

The village of **Kolofana** has tavernas and a few rooms. Once the bread is delivered, the bus continues to the road's end, reversing into a convenient driveway beside the bright, clean and well-maintained monastery of **Agia Paraskevi**. The feast day here is on July 26th, when pilgrims stay in the rooms which stretch in a line beside the church. Follow the locals down a short dirt track to the small, scrubbly cove of **Paradission**: a misleading name, as the beach itself is poor and tiny, though the setting is picturesque. A few tumbledown houses lie abandoned around the bay. A little jetty makes a good diving point into the sea and some shade is provided by the low cliff. There is a pleasing view across to **Gramvoussa** island - which incidentally is reputed to have Amorgos' best beaches! Unless you have your own boat, you are unlikely to be able to take advantage of them, although were you to stay in Kolofana you could doubtless pay a fisherman to take you there.

Other beaches in this area are better than that at Paradission, but require more than the three hour stay which the bus allows. If you are Kolofana-based and have time, a path takes off from near the monastery - head a few metres down the road towards Kolofana, then turn on to the dirt track which passes between the group of houses on the right of the road. It is forty minutes' walk to the first cove, **Ormos Liveros**, where a liner, the Olympia, ran aground. Twenty minutes further down the same path leads to

Ormos Kalotaritissa, a protected cove with a fairly good, small beach.

From Kolofana village itself, a track leads north to the bay of Ormos Katokampos and another beach - but watch out for the sea-urchins.

Back at Paradission, across the street from the bus pull up, is a low, barn-like kafe-taverna. The friendly old owner mostly makes salads, but can be persuaded to cook a meal, and bus passengers congregate here before returning to Katapola.

AEGIALI
Getting There
See Katapola.

The northern port of Aegiali is smaller than Katapola, and more attractive in many ways. It is set in a bay of steep cliffs, with a great rock of an island, Nikiria, at the western edge, almost joined to the Amorgos coast. Together with the distant outline of Donoussa island, this makes for spectacular sunsets.

Aegiali has a long, golden sandy beach, backed by fertile fields, in a valley which narrows to a steep gorge below Langada.

In 1988 Aegiali experienced severe water shortage problems. The water 'ran out' four times that summer - on one occasion there was no water for fifteen consecutive days! The reason for this was apparently that the previous year's water had not been paid for, in full, and the water supply boat relegated Aegiali to the bottom of its list of priorities! Let's hope the relevant authorities pay up, in the future....

Accommodation
A fairer deal here, than in Katapola, and the standard is better. Room owners meet the boats, but before checking in, verify the number of bars, cafes and tavernas in the vicinity. The narrow stepped street, running up beside the ridiculously overpriced and ugly Hotel Mike, to the Restaurant Korali, has many rooms, but is a very noisy area, due to one or two objectionable bars which play amplified music, more suited to Stringfellows than Aegiali. This continues until around 0400hrs, so don't expect much sleep! Happily, they also close around the beginning of September. Of these noisy rooms, those over the Mageia Cafe are pleasant, and if you find one at the back, and close the windows, the noise hardly penetrates! These small rooms are spotlessly clean, well equipped and nicely furnished. The woman who runs them meets the ferries and is very helpful.

Other less rowdy accommodation can be found by following the beachside road a little further, and heading back into the main town past the church - the bakery, for one, has pleasant rooms. If you want a beach based holiday, follow the road around the back of the bay to the far end, where there are a few pensions and the very pleasant Pension/Hotel Askas - a little more expensive than the rooms, but with private bathrooms, and balconies overlooking the sea. The hotel has its own taverna and serves breakfast. There are also a few rooms in the villages of Langada and Tholaria.

Camping In an attempt to decrease the numbers of tourists sleeping on the beach, the village authorities have installed a campsite behind the beach, with a little shade, a little water, and a little electricity! These latter two luxuries are only available on an unreliable basis. The prices at this basic facility are no lower than the usual Greek campsite, so perhaps it is not surprising that people continue to wild camp on the beach, although it is a pity, especially when they ignore the villagers' "no topless" signs, and continue to undress in full view! Is this fair? I doubt most 'Brits' would brave local reaction on their own coastline! Imagine going topless or sleeping out on Blackpool beach....

Food and Drink

There is less of a selection here, than in Katapola, but the two tavernas To Limani and To Korali cater well enough. They are augmented by a few kafe-tavernas - the Mageia Kafe, up the steps past the Hotel Mike, is one of those which plays over-loud music at night. However, it is excellently situated for breakfasts, and has a wide variety of offerings, including fresh fruit salad, yoghurt with nuts and honey, fruit juice and lots of gooey cakes. The initially rather indifferent attitude of the owners thaws with time....

There are a couple of kafe/tavernas on the beach - the waiters at the Selini speak English, but it is a little trendy, and the local kafe, just prior to the Selini, may prove preferable. Here they also serve Mr Softy type ice-cream cones, chocolate and vanilla....

The best taverna at this end of the island is in Langada village.

Vital Information

Aegiali is smaller than Katapola. It has no bank, but the postman changes money when he visits town, three times a week! Everyone recommends his services, but in fact he can be difficult to locate. An alternative is George, who runs the souvenir shop on the right of the street, just before the beach. He displays a sign: "Information Office", and helps tourists with rooms, donkey hire (yes...), postage stamps et al - he speaks fluent English. However, he reduces his services drastically during August, when the 'tourists are of a bad kind' and waste his time by asking stupid questions!

The alternative place for exchange is the post office, in Langada. This building is marked by a sign outside, and is up a flight of stairs in someone's living room. It has a metered telephone, and when questioned about opening hours, they say, "We're always here!"

The police station is also in Langada, and transport there is fairly regular - the Aegiali bus, which arrived on the scene in 1986, serves the two communities of Langada and Tholaria, throughout the day until midnight. There is no moped hire, and it is not necessary. Donkeys can be hired from either the Selini Kafe, by the beach, or a couple of locals. Ask at George's souvenir shop for details, make reservations in advance, and prepare to be annoyed when the farmer decides he has a vine crop to gather, which he forgot about when you made your agreement!

Connections with the Chora, to the south, can be made by a van which travels there twice daily, morning and evening, though only in peak season.

Otherwise it's the ferries, or possibly a lift on the twice weekly school bus, which takes High School children from the north to the south on Monday morning, and brings them back again Friday night.

Aegiali has a ferry boat ticket office, just before the church, in a general store which has a wide variety of goods for sale. The same store has a metered telephone... but getting a line out is nigh on impossible...   so what's new?

The bakery is up the hill, and signposted all over town. The baker sells cold bottled water, which can become vital during a water shortage. Beyond his shop, to the right, is the clinic with the doctor and pharmacy.

Beaches
They are much better than those in the south. The village beach is extremely long and sandy, and extends right around the bay. Continuing still further, a footpath leads to a series of smaller, sandy coves directly across the bay from the ferry boat quay.

Sites to See
See Excursions.

Excursions
Langada   This is the prettiest village on the island. It also has the best taverna, which also provides Langada's only accommodation.

Buses leave every couple of hours or so from Aegiali, otherwise it is a forty five minute walk up the hill, on the donkey track which cuts through the shady olive groves to the bottom of the village.

The bus stops on the main road, from where a path leads into the main square at the top of Langada. Around this are a kafe, two general stores, and the police station. The path to the left leads down the hill between stunningly bright white walls, passing the post office, towards the bottom of the village, where Nikos' bougainvillea-hung, taverna terrace commands a lovely view of the fertile valley below.

The rooms (tel 73310) which are new, with balcony space and en suite showers, enter the expensively rated category, but remember this is Amorgos, and thus excellent value for money. Nikos' food is imaginative, a virtue not found in all Greek tavernas; it is delicious and well cooked. He also doubles as the village baker, making bread early in the morning.

Not far from Nikos' taverna is another general store, with a metered telephone and facility for changing money. The wife of the owner is English, and her three children speak English.

One could happily while away a few days in the white peace of Langada, and there are a number of interesting walks radiating from the village. The most straightforward is down to the nearby, ruined settlement of Stroumbos. Follow the low path, which heads up the valley, along the edge of the gorge (unfortunately used as the village tip) until it crosses the narrow mouth of a crevice. **Stroumbos**, which was inhabited up to fifteen years ago, is clearly visible; the two white houses have been restored by foreign families. The locals had a neat description of Stroumbos, in more prosperous times - 'a village of twelve houses and thirteen bread ovens'!

The path continues   right around the back of the valley across to the opposite village of Tholaria - this circular donkey track continues from Tholaria back down to Aegiali, and used to serve as the main thoroughfare. The 'main' roads were constructed only a few years ago, to prepare for the arrival of the bus.

Another somewhat more arduous walk leads to the chapel of **Agios Theologos**. Take the uphill path from outside Langada's main square, passing, on the left, a broad path to **Panagia Church**. The steep climb to Theologos takes about forty five minutes, but is worth it, if only for the view. Islanders claim that on a clear day it is possible to see the great monastery of Patmos, which may be why the chapel was built on this spot. It was apparently constructed during the 5th century, one source says with stones from Milos. If that is true, one wonders why. Amorgos has plenty of its own stones.

Continuing on the same path, which soon becomes little more than a goat track, leads, eventually, to **Stavros Church**, from where a path to the west climbs up to Chorafakia, Amorgos' highest mountain, at 821m. Another path presses on around the peak and down to the sea, at the site of tin mines abandoned in 1943.

Tholaria Situated on the mountain across the gorge from Langada, Tholaria is picturesque, but not so pretty as Langada. It has a large, impressive church, four tavernas, the largest of which, just below the church, serves good food and has rooms.

The bus regularly connects Tholaria with Aegiali, but it is also a pleasant, thirty minute walk up the donkey track from the port. The village has a very agricultural atmosphere, with mule troughs, chicken coops and stables squeezed in between the houses which line the main street. Above the village, row upon row of terraces, dotted with the occasional threshing floor, stretch away into the distance.

The village apparently took its name from nearby, vaulted 'tholos' - tombs dating from the Roman period.

Island Customs, Feasts, Specialities and History

Religious Festivals Amorgos' most significant feast day is on November 21st at the Chozoviotissa monastery, when the presentation of the Virgin Mary is celebrated. The festival of Agios Giorgos Balsamitis, near Katapola, takes place on April 23rd, and on July 26th there is the feast of Agios Paraskevi, near Kolofana.

Religious festivals on the south of the island include: August 15th, the festival of Panagia; 14th of September, the feast of Agios Stavros, in the mountains; November 13th, the festival of Agios Yiannis, and the 8th of December, at the church of Agios Nikolaos in Aegiali.

Wedding Customs Even today, island weddings are carried out with great gusto. On the day before the ceremony, village women come to the couple's future home and make up the marriage bed. The youngest child present is tossed on to the bed, to encourage fertility, and the women also throw rice, almonds and money.

The couple are not supposed to meet on the night before the nuptials. On the wedding day morning musicians call at the homes of the bride and groom, to take them to church. During the ceremony, the rings are switched from the left hand, where they are worn throughout the engagement, to the right. Afterwards, the musicians lead a procession back to the new home, where the bride and groom and their parents greet the guests, handing out almonds as favours. Wedding cakes include pastelli, and xerotigano, the latter being a dough made of flour and water, and fried in honey.

The party takes place in the village square, frequently with a goat being roasted and most of the village attending as guests. Afterwards, the priest returns to their house and blesses it, waving incense around the rooms.

The following morning the musicians return to wake up the couple and take them to a breakfast, which often includes soup from the remains of the goat. Dancing continues throughout the day.

Local Produce Foods typical of the island are a pastelli cake. This is made with honey and sesame seeds, and lemon slices are placed between the pieces when it is cut. This cake is brought out on special occasions, particularly at weddings and christenings.

Amorgos also specialises in a cheese called mithira, and in locally grown herbs. Are herbs uniquely abundant on Amorgos (and if so, why?), or does one simply hear less about them in other places? I'm not sure, but the German owner of one of the tourist shops in Aegiali, Gitti Roth, has made the most of the cornucopia, stocking some thirty seven different herbs, from camomile to capers, and marjoram to monkpepper. She also publishes an interesting leaflet which lists the uses for each herb. Her shop is a tribute to the glorious scents of the Greek countryside.

History The island had three ancient city states during the Cycladic period - **Minoa** (for which Katapola served as the harbour) is the remains of one of these, probably settled by people from Naxos, though the Amorgots like to believe in a Minoan connection. The city took shape around 2000 BC, although in the bay of Katapola, excavations have uncovered many graves dating back as far as 3000 BC. The marble idols contained in these graves are now in the National Museum in Athens.

The other two city states were **Kastri** (now Arkesini) and ancient **Aegiali**, of which very little remains.

Ptolemy of Egypt ruled the island for a period, and the Alexandrian Gods of Isis and Serapis were worshipped. Settlers from Samos arrived in the 7th century BC, bringing with them cult worship of the goddess Hera, although Apollo, Aphrodite, Artemis and Zeus were also revered. Later, the Romans used Amorgos as a place of exile, and thereafter continued the usual Greek island story of one ruler after another, down through the centuries.

The Venetians built the Kastro in the 13th century, after the departure of the Crusaders. In 1537 the Turks took control, and the Russians ruled for a period during the 18th century. One feature peculiar to Amorgos was the fame of the island's embroidery, which spread far and wide during the 17th-19th centuries. Apparently some is on display at the Victoria and Albert Museum, in London. The island's women weavers were also famous for a fine red cloth dyed with plants and seashells.

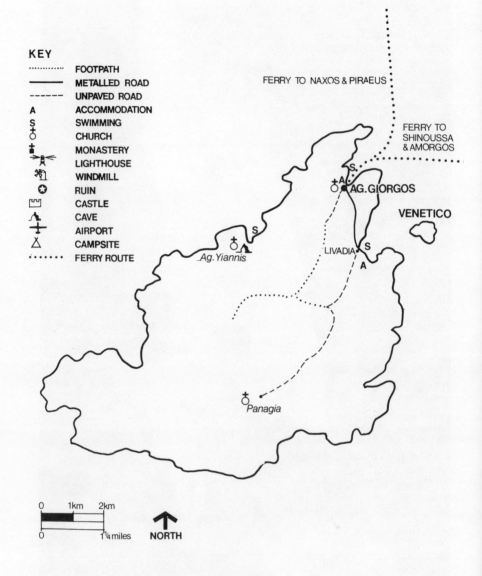

KEY

·············	FOOTPATH
———	METALLED ROAD
- - - - -	UNPAVED ROAD
A	ACCOMMODATION
S	SWIMMING
☦	CHURCH
☩	MONASTERY
⚓	LIGHTHOUSE
🗼	WINDMILL
✪	RUIN
⌂	CASTLE
⌂	CAVE
✈	AIRPORT
⛺	CAMPSITE
···········	FERRY ROUTE

FERRY TO NAXOS & PIRAEUS

FERRY TO SHINOUSSA & AMORGOS

S

A AG.GIORGOS

VENETICO

S

Ag.Yiannis

LIVADIA S

A

Panagia

0	1km	2km
0		1¼miles

NORTH

Illustration 2 Iraklia island

CHAPTER THREE   IRAKLIA

On a scale of 1 to 5:	Sites to visit: 2
Appeal: 3	Accessibility: 2
Exploitation: 1	
Beaches: 4	
Scenic Beauty: 3	Population :100
Accommodation - standard: 3	Telephone prefix: 0285
Accommodation - availability: 3	Size: Approximately 6km wide
Facilities: 1	and 9km from top to bottom.

Location
Approximately 6km due south of the most adjacent portion of Naxos island
(though about 50km by sea from that island's port), and 30km west of
Amorgos. Despite Iraklia being around 20km north-east of Ios, there is no
ferry route between the two.

Getting There
Airport: No.

Ferries: The following comments apply not only to Iraklia, but to the
nearby islands of Shinoussa and Koufonisi.
   Transport direct from Piraeus is not particularly convenient - there are
about three connections a week. However, besides the long haul ferries that
call, the island is serviced by a local craft based at Amorgos. Its route is:
Amorgos (Katapola), Koufonisi, Shinoussa, Iraklia, Naxos and back, four
times a week in summer - which means day trips to these places are a
possibility.
   Docking at Iraklia is towards the end of a fairly deep inlet, with room for
only one boat at the quay. Disembarking can be 'interesting' if there
happens to be another ship in port, and may involve scrambling over the
deck of an earlier arrival!

General
Iraklia is the least developed and the most peaceful of a little group of four
islets, spaced out between Naxos and Amorgos. It has two villages, each
with about fifty inhabitants: Agios Giorgos at the port, and Panagia, the
capital, some 3km inland, on the mountainside. The settlements are linked
by a partly paved road, but there is no public transport. This appealing
island is small, tranquil and friendly, and is blessed with two excellent,
sandy beaches.
   It is five minutes walk from the quayside into Agios Giorgos, and the
road divides where it enters the village, on either side of a dried up
river-bed. The right fork leads towards the focal Kafe Melissa, while the
left turning twists between the houses to head off for Livadi beach and
Panagia. Although obviously fulfilling the role of 'The Chora', Panagia is
never referred to as such on Iraklia.

Accommodation

The island has around thirty rooms for tourists. These fill up in mid-season but are usually empty by August 17th. Enthusiastically, room owners meet the boats, one wearing a T-shirt which advertises her rooms and hot water, in four languages. Accommodation varies from cheap and basic (the few old-fashioned rooms in Agios Giorgos) to reasonable and comfortable. The Kafe Melissa has three (basic) rooms for rent, and serves many other functions. Most of the newer rooms are built on the outskirts of the tiny port, along the road towards Livadi beach and Panagia.

The new taverna on Livadi beach has two rooms, sharing a bathroom. They have electricity and solar heated water, but tend towards the expensive, considering the situation, which is ideal but very remote. There is no accommodation in Panagia.

Camping Iraklia has no campsite. The best place to 'pound in the pegs' is Livadi beach, with its two convenient tavernas - though perhaps you should eat at the one which doesn't have rooms!

Food and Drink

Agios Giorgos has five tavernas - a couple of old fashioned ones in the village, and three more along the road to Livadi. Prices are reasonable, even if variety is limited by the ferry boat supplies. The tavernas at Livadi beach serve food, but there are no tavernas up in Panagia.

Vital Information

There is no bank, so visitors should exchange their money before leaving Athens or Naxos. Nor is there a post office - the Kafe-Taverna Melissa doubles as a post office, along with everything else - at least, this is where the mail gets sorted, and there's a post box on the wall. The kafe also houses the island's telephone and serves as the port's only general store.

Panagia has two general stores, and a wood-fired bakery. The bread for the port is trucked down daily to the Kafe Melissa. The doctor can also be located here: he holds clinics alternately in the port and Panagia.

Iraklia has no: policeman, ferry boat office, island map, or public transport. This lack of buses means that to get to Panagia it is necessary to walk, to hitch a lift with one of the island's few agricultural vehicles, or to catch the bread van, which returns to Panagia daily, at around 1130hrs. (Wait at the junction where the Panagia road leaves town for Livadi beach and Panagia - or ask at the Kafe Melissa.) In the evening the van often travels down again to meet up with the ferry, as bread is shipped from Iraklia to the neighbouring island of Shinoussa.

Beaches

The island's two best beaches also happen to be the most accessible. The clean, sandy port beach, backed by a small vineyard and shaded by tamarisk trees, is a perfect place to swim. More spectacular, due to its size, is Livadi, over the low hill to the east of the port, on **Mourto Bay**. This sweeping beach, also of sand, has two new tavernas (one with rooms), and a few trees for shade. Climbing the path at the far side of Livadi beach leads

over the hill to the wilder, less attractive but even more remote beach of
Tou Korigadou.
Incidentally, the sea around Iraklia, and the neighbouring islands, is
surprisingly cold, which is apparently due to a number of cross-currents in
the area.
The island does have other beaches, but they are difficult to reach.
Aliminia cove is a three hour walk via Panagia, and located on the
north-west coast, near the chapel of Agios Yiannis. This church's feast day
is celebrated each year, on August 28th, when all the islanders arrive by
boat. Visitors present on that date, might just get a lift!
Although there are no organized boat trips to any of Iraklia's other
beaches, a fisherman named Kleanthis, who lives in Agios Giorgos, deposits
tourists on sandy strips of their choice, or his recommendation. His tiny
blue and white boat, 'Anoula', bobs about, moored to the fishing boat jetty
near the beach. Ask at the Kafe Melissa for his whereabouts, and agree on
the price before you set off! His caique bucks about in the slightest breeze.
It is reassuring to know that when the boat was new, in 1971, Kleanthis
sailed her to Iraklia single-handed, all the way from Spetses, a non-stop
journey of some twenty-two hours. Kleanthis and his doughty Anoula also
makes crossings to neighbouring Shinoussa, for a fee...

Sites to See
Iraklia has one outstanding natural attraction - a great cave in the hills of
the west coast, not far from Agios Yiannis chapel and Aliminia beach.
However, the cave, named 'Agios Yiannis' after the chapel, has not been
the subject of any tourist development. It can be reached by a two hour
walk, due north from Panagia, but it is probably a better idea to try and pay
an islander to act as a guide, or to travel by boat.
The entrance to the cave is the size of a doorway, beyond which it opens
out into a large chamber with stalagmites and stalactites. Islanders claim
that after the famous Dirrou caves in the Peloponnese, and the equally
famous caves near Yannina, this is the best cave in Greece. (Well, they
would...).

Excursions
The walk to Panagia can be made by two different routes. The main road,
which is more direct, continues up the hillside beyond Livadi beach, and is
paved in places. The alternative is to follow the main street of Agios
Giorgos inland, beyond the second big church. This road loops around and
eventually meets up with the other road, about three-quarters of the way to
Panagia. Also see Beaches.

Island Customs, Feasts, Specialities and History
Religious Festivals Both the churches in the port have festivals: the church
of Agios Giorgos, in the centre of the village, celebrates St George's Day,
on April 23rd, and the feast day of the second church, Taxiarchis, is on
November 8th. Panagia church, in Panagia, has its 'yiorti' on August 15th.
Diminutive as it is, Iraklia was mentioned by Homer as having sent
twenty ships to Troy.

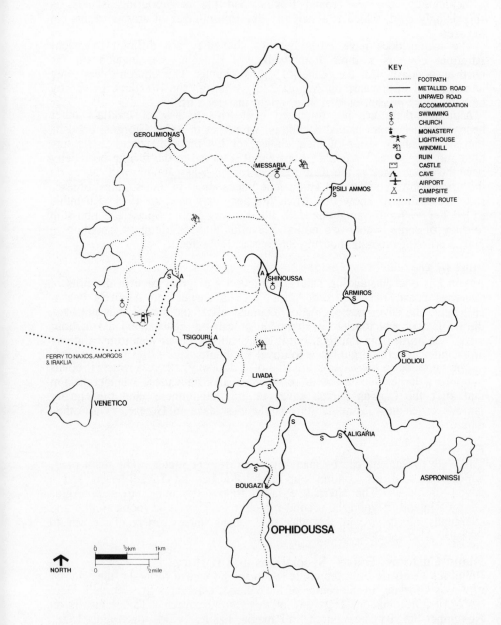

GEROLIMIONAS
S

MESSARIA

PSILI AMMOS
S

SHINOUSSA

ARMIROS
S

TSIGOURI A
S

LIVADA
S

LIOLIOU
S

FERRY TO NAXOS, AMORGOS & IRAKLIA

VENETICO

ALIGARIA
S

ASPRONISSI

BOUGAZI

OPHIDOUSSA

NORTH

0   ½km   1km

0   ½mile

Illustration 3 Shinoussa island

SHINOUSSA

On a scale of 1 to 5: Appeal: 3 Exploitation: 2 Beaches: 4 Scenic Beauty: 3 Accommodation - standard: 2 Accommodation - availability: 3 Facilities: 2	Sites to visit: 1 Accessibility: 2 Population :190 (and falling) Telephone prefix: 0285 Size: Approximately 6½m long and 4km wide.

Location
3km north-east of Iraklia.

Getting There
Airport: No.

Ferries See Iraklia. Iraklia and Shinoussa are so close that it is possible to travel between the two by caique or even hitching a lift on a yacht.

General
From the lone ferry boat quay it is a hot and very dusty fifteen minute uphill climb to Shinoussa town. The road appears to have been abandoned half-way through its construction, and the shortest route is up an old path, which involves climbing over water pipes, trenches and mounds of dirt. The capital, Shinoussa or Panagia, is a long, strung out village, straggling down a narrow main street, a short distance from the sea.

It is not too surprising that the traveller's first impression of the island can be rather dubious, particularly if arriving in the middle of the night. But Shinoussa's inhabitants welcome visitors with naive delight, beaches abound, and, after a short while, most misgivings evaporate.

Gradually, modernization is coming to the island: electricity arrived in 1984, the number of telephones - currently three - is due to be extended to forty, and the ferry boat quay is undergoing slow, very slow, enlargement. Most people live in Panagia, the only other settlement being Messaria, 4km away, with twenty inhabitants.

Efforts are clearly being made to attract visitors and tourism may well be the island's only possible future. The population is rapidly dwindling, mainly because the economy is based on agriculture, and no young islander gladly embraces the idea of eking out a living from the stony wheat fields, which cover most of Shinoussa's surface. However, farming still dominates, for the present, and there are tractors, threshing floors and mules beside every track and on every hillside.

The island has a junior school but by 1990 there won't be any children of school age. In the 1940s, there were around eighty five pupils.

Accommodation
Shinoussa has about sixty, well advertised rooms, most of them along the main road of Panagia. Rooms Potiti, on the left at the outset of the street, is run by a friendly woman who is prepared to bargain over prices. It is a fairly modern, reasonably priced choice, with shared bathrooms and intermittent hot water. Cheaper but more basic accommodation can be found at several of the cafes further along the street.

There are also two modern blocks of rooms alongside the harbour, one set in a lovely orchard/garden, the other serving food. Although both look attractive, they are rather 'out of it', especially since the harbour cove does not have a good beach.

Camping Shinoussa has no organised campsite, although there is talk of a site at Livadi bay. The latter certainly is, a reasonable place to camp, as is the olive grove in the bay of Mersini, where the ferries dock.

Food and Drink
As so often happens on these small islands, one energetic and far-sighted proprietor puts himself out to help tourists. In this case, your man is the owner of the pizzeria, at the far end of the village street, on the left. His establishment offers a wide selection of reasonably priced food, from toasted sandwiches and pizzas, to 'full-blown' Greek meals.

There are other possibilities for eating out - numerous small kafe-tavernas along the same main street, but in general their choice is much more limited than at the pizzeria.

Vital Information
As aforementioned, the pizzeria owner is the person to turn to in times of need. He speaks English and can be persuaded to exchange currency, but this should really be organised before arriving, because the island has no banks. There is a post office but it is not be be relied upon for exchange. In fact, it is located in somebody's living room, and is signposted up a short track   off the main road, near the harbour-end of the village. The one public telephone is across the street from the post office, down a few steps, in a cave-like room. I wouldn't rely on that either!

The doctor, whose clinic doubles as a pharmacy, is to be found in the square, modern building at the outset of the road to Messaria, not far from the church.

There is no police station (nor crime), no port police, no public transport, no disco and no bakery. Bread comes from Naxos or Iraklia. The pizzeria owner used to 'quadruple' as a baker, but not surprisingly, he found it too much work. Incidentally, he also sells island maps but if he runs out of them, there is a useful map painted on a board in the main street, next door to the telephone office. Across the street from his restaurant is a hillbilly type store with a sign, tied to the fence, boasting, "We sell everything you want. CIGARETTES". Other general stores range along the high street, and the cafes also stock foodstuffs. There is a ferry boat ticket office, immediately prior to the

High Street pizzeria but it only opens in the evenings. Ferry boat timetables are pinned up outside.

Beaches
Shinoussa is certainly not lacking in this facility, boasting a total of nineteen different beaches. However, despite the quantity, the island doesn't appear to have any one beach which quite rivals, for example, Finikas on Koufonisi, or Livadi on nearby Iraklia. The best beach, **Tsigouri**, happens to be the closest to the town. To get there, select the first road to the right after entering the village from the port. The sandy, tree shaded beach is ten minutes walk down the winding track. It has one taverna, with a few basic rooms, and, in the height of season, windsurfing hire, and water skiing.

Other beaches, close to Shinoussa, are Livadi and Almiros: to reach them, continue on the main street out of the town (in the opposite direction from the port). The road, now a track, divides among wheat fields, and the right fork twists and turns down to the long, narrow, rather scrubby beach of **Livadi**, about fifteen minutes walk away. Signs of development are visible in a peculiar stone construction on the far hillside. This resembles an ancient theatre, but is actually a modern, water retaining device. A British company is constructing a holiday complex but, according to the islanders, work has been continuing for years and years, with little progress.

Beyond Livadi beach, over the neck of the headland, are three more sandy coves, at **Aligaria**.

Back at the main track, the left fork leads towards **Almiros** beach. Turn off at the first track on the left, climb over the wall, where the track ends, and follow the path, between fields grazed by herds of goats, and over a stile to the sea. This is a wild and windy cove with little shelter, and a small beach. The main track eventually reaches a better beach at **Lioliou**.

The beach at **Psili Ammos, near Messaria**, is well recommended. It is about fifteen minutes walk to the east of the village. Heading west from Messaria leads to the cove of **Gerolimionas**, and another beach.

Sites to See/Excursions
See Beaches.

Island Customs, Feasts, Specialities and History
Religious Festivals The two major fiestas on the island take place on August 15th, at Panagia church, in Panagia (Shinoussa), and at the church of Theotokou, on March 25th, in Messaria.

The only 'speciality', for which Shinoussa is noted (at least by the Shinoussians), is a variety of mastic bush. Mastic is the basis of chewing gum, and grows in great profusion on Chios, in the north-east Aegean.

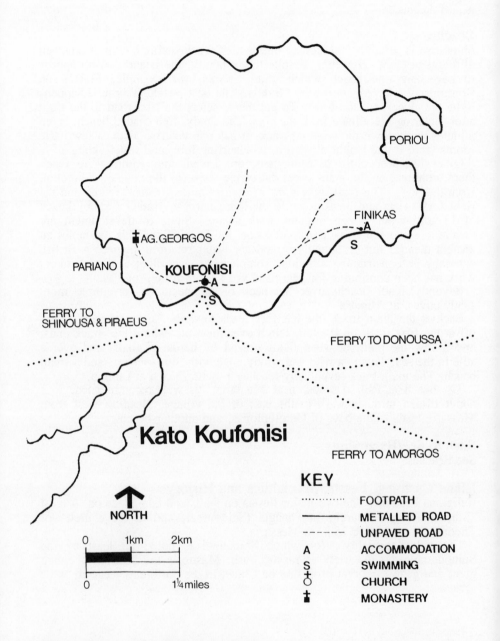

POROIOU

FINIKAS
A
S

AG. GEORGOS

PARIANO

KOUFONISI
A
S

FERRY TO
SHINOUSA & PIRAEUS

FERRY TO DONOUSSA

Kato Koufonisi

FERRY TO AMORGOS

NORTH

0   1km   2km

0   1¼ miles

KEY

.... FOOTPATH

—————— METALLED ROAD

– – – – – UNPAVED ROAD

A   ACCOMMODATION

S   SWIMMING

☩○   CHURCH

⬛   MONASTERY

Illustration 4 Koufonisi island

KOUFONISI & KEROS

On a scale of 1 to 5:	Sites to visit: 1
Appeal: 4	Accessibility: 2
Exploitation: 2	Alternative names:Koufonisi,
Beaches: 4	Koufonisos
Scenic Beauty: 3	Population : 240
Accommodation - standard: 2	Telephone prefix: 0285
Accommodation - availability: 2	Size: 5m wide and 4km from north
Facilities: 2	to south.

Location
Set down in between the islands of Naxos and Amorgos, Koufonisi is only 5km from the uninhabited east shore of Naxos, and some 22km north-west of Amorgos.

Getting There
Airport: No.

Ferries: See Iraklia. A new quay was completed some years ago, turning Koufonisi town into the island port. However, it is a breezy harbour, sharing the currents and cold water of the nearby islets. In bad weather boats have to dock at the old port of **Pariano**, just over the low-rise to the west of the main town.

General
Actually two islands, Ano ('Upper') Koufonisi and Kato ('Lower') Koufonisi, which are separated by a narrow channel. Kato Koufonisi is virtually uninhabited; a summertime home to a couple of families, with no towns or villages. By contrast, Ano Koufonisi ('Koufonisi'), which is extremely low-lying, barely raising its shoulders above the waves, has a thriving population.

Koufonisi has always been the administrative centre of this island group (Koufonisi, Iraklia, Shinoussa and Donoussa), and is the most developed. Although numbers of tourists remain relatively low, visitors are arriving faster than buildings are being erected. With an indigenous population of two hundred and forty, Koufonisi can appear overcrowded in high season.

Unlike its neighbours, the island has only experienced minimal depopulation over recent decades. This can be explained by the fact that the economy is based on fish, rather than agriculture and a fleet of forty fishing caiques maintains the island's prosperity. This is in direct contrast to nearby Shinoussa, for example, where the economy has traditionally been supported by farming. As a result Shinoussa is now in serious danger of becoming totally deserted.

The reasons for fishing prospering, vis-a-vis farming, are obvious: fish are in great demand, thus expensive, and marketable, as far away as

Athens; island farming is laborious, inefficient and disproportionately time-consuming. Few young people now wish to farm, but consider fishing a much more viable prospect.

Unusually, the bay is full of fishing boats lying at anchor, rather than tied to the quayside.

Accommodation

Reasonably priced accommodation is scattered around the harbour and the town beach, with quite a number of modern pension blocks. The other options are at Finikas beach, which is about a twenty minute walk from the port, along a partly paved track, starting out from beyond the town beach. Here are several rooms, which fill up in the summer, as do the island's two hundred beds. Most visitors are Greeks, or foreigners 'in the know'.

Camping There is no official campsite, as yet, but most people informally camp at Finikas. Here the owner of the taverna has provided showers and toilets for campers (and tables where they can eat his meals, of course!).

Food and Drink

The tavernas are concentrated around the town beach, and there are the two at Finikas. Prices are very reasonable, but the choice is often rather restricted. In fact, some establishments run out of food, towards the end of the evening - another example of too many tourists on too small an island!

Vital Information

There are no banks, but the post office exchanges money. The latter is situated on the town's main thoroughfare. The OTE office, open 0800-1500hrs, borders the same main road, almost opposite the post office, as does the ferry boat ticket office, with timetables on display.

The town boasts a police station, whose one officer is also responsible for law and order on the islands of Iraklia, Shinoussa, and Donoussa. The doctor used to fill a similar multi-island role, but now each community has its own medic.

The village has a bakery, and a few stores but no public transport, nor moped hire, to date.

Beaches

The town beach looks good enough, but Koufonisi is also blessed with Finikas Bay, one of the best places to swim in the Aegean. In actual fact there are three beaches edging the bay, one after the other, all sandy, wide and golden. Shade is provided by a few backshore trees. The name Finikas means 'palm tree' and indeed there is a palm tree to complete the scene.

There are a couple of inferior coves at Pariano bay, near the chapel of Agios Giorgos, and a good beach near Cape Poriou, about one hour's walk north-east of the village - keep following the 'main street' until it becomes a track. But most people find Finikas more than adequate!

Excursions

Greeks go to Koufonisi to fish, and it is possible to rent a caique for a fishing trip. There is also an excursion to Kato Koufonisi, and small boats make the crossing daily. Kato Koufonisi has three beaches, but they do not compare with Finikas.

KEROS

Population: 0.

This uninhabited island is situated south-east of Koufonisi. There are no villages, only a few goatherds and their animals. The goats are often left alone for long periods to graze on the scrubby vegetation.

Some sources quote a population of ten, but these are not permanent residents. However, the island was settled in ancient times, and two important marble statues (The Harpist and the Flautist), found in a tomb dating back to around 2500 BC, are in the Athens National Museum.

South of Keros are the two uninhabited islands, **Antikeros** and **Drima**.

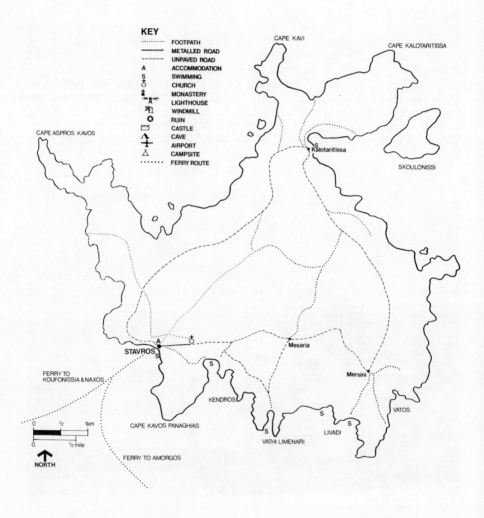

KEY
········· FOOTPATH
———— METALLED ROAD
‒ ‒ ‒ ‒ UNPAVED ROAD
A ACCOMMODATION
S SWIMMING
⊙ CHURCH
⚑ MONASTERY
A LIGHTHOUSE
🕍 WINDMILL
❂ RUIN
[▥] CASTLE
⚑ CAVE
✈ AIRPORT
△ CAMPSITE
··········· FERRY ROUTE

CAPE KAVI

CAPE KALOTARITISSA

CAPE ASPROS KAVOS

S
Kalotaritissa

SKOULONISSI

A
STAVROS
S

Mesaria

Mersini

FERRY TO
KOUFONISSIA & NAXOS

S

S

KENDROS

VATOS

S

0   ½   1km

CAPE KAVOS PANAGHIAS

S

LIVADI

S

0   ½ mile

VATHI LIMENARI

↑
NORTH

FERRY TO AMORGOS

Illustration 5 Donoussa island

DONOUSSA

On a scale of 1 to 5:	Sites to visit: 2
Appeal: 4	Accessibility: 1
Exploitation: 1	
Beaches: 4	Population 225
Scenic Beauty: 3	Telephone prefix: 0285
Accommodation - standard: 2	Size: Approximately 7km from
Accommodation - availability: 3	north to south, and 6km from
Facilities: 1	east to west.

Location
Set down between Naxos and Amorgos, but more northerly than the Iraklia, Shinoussa, Koufonisi group. Donoussa is about 23km northwest of Amorgos, and 15km east of Naxos.

Getting There
Airport: No.

Ferries: The big inter-island ferries call two or three times a week, in each direction, in high season, but less frequently at other times. These tend to be long haul type ferries, so a journey has to be well planned. They dock at the newly extended quay which projects in a semi-circular sweep from the portside village.
   The Amorgos based supply boat/ferry (currently the FB Skopelitis) includes Donoussa on its schedule, twice a week: its route is Amorgos (both ports), Donoussa, Koufonisi, Shinoussa, Iraklia, Naxos, and back the same way, on the same day. Thus a day trip to Donoussa from Amorgos is possible, although the island warrants a longer stay than that. (Note that this craft calls at Donoussa less frequently than at Koufonisi, et al).
   Unlike the large boats, the local ferry persists in docking at the old jetty, close by the waterfront taverna. This makes for easier unloading of supplies, but inevitably confuses passengers who may have arrived at one place but are destined to depart from the other! Also note that while the FB Skopelitis is boarded from the stern on most islands, here it is entered from the bow.
   Presuming you disembark successfully, bear in mind that transport problems are increased by the combination of windy weather and dangerous currents, which can make the seas around Donoussa very choppy. In winter the island is frequently cut off for up to fifteen days at a time; even in the summer there are days when the boats can't dock, so remember to allow plenty of time for connections.

General
Donoussa is a wild, rough little jewel of a place, with some fabulous sandy beaches and just enough facilities to allow for a very pleasant stay indeed.

It has my vote for the most captivating of the island group between Amorgos and Naxos.

Over the course of the past decade, the island has struggled into the 20th century. Electricity and running water were installed in 1981. A new OTE office arrived and, in 1988, the completion of a ferry boat quay enabled, for the first time ever, large ferries to dock directly.

Mind you, the luxuries of electric light do not extend to outlying villages, which are linked to the main port of Stavros by a rough, steep donkey track. Surely these hamlets will be deserted within the next decade - a prophecy which the electricity company must also have made. Despite the overall island population steadily declining since the war, it has stabilised in recent years.

Most supplies have to be brought in by boat, although there are springs at Mersini, where fruit and vegetables are produced. Exploration continues for water sources. The island has eight children in its junior school, but no high school, or functioning priest - the old man who sits at the waterfront taverna is retired. When a priest is deemed necessary, one is 'shipped' over from Amorgos.

Accommodation

In peak season all forty of Donoussa's available beds may be filled. But by August 20th, there should be plenty of space.

The only advertised rooms (tel 9584793) are behind the church/town hall area. The best plan for first-time visitors is to head for the Blue Lagoon Cafe, which is atop the bakery near the quay and entered from the street at the rear. The young Greek owner speaks English and is apparently out to make his fortune. As such, he is extremely keen to help tourists, and in a disinterested fashion too, being willing to locate rooms, direct you about the island, and answer any questions. Having said that, his breakfasts are not cheap, but as this is one of those 'food-is-hard-to-come-by-islands', you have to be prepared to pay.

Rooms vary, in price and condition, from inexpensive to reasonable. A few don't have any running water and most lack hot water.

Camping There is no campsite, but wild camping is tolerated on Kendros beach, over the hill from the main port. A word of warning is not to camp (or wander around topless) on the village beach.

Food and Drink

All establishments are totally dependent on the ferry - on occasions the local boat struggles to dock under the burden of supplies it brings to Donoussa! This is no exaggeration - just watch!

The aforementioned Blue Lagoon Cafe is an excellent location for breakfast, with its tables spread across the roof, allowing a bird's eye view of the harbourside activities. For lunch, join everyone else at the local, 'genuine-article' Kafe Taverna To Kyma, which is perched just above the harbour. They serve good, though not particularly varied, cooked food. The Taverna Meltemi, near the beach, is also attractive, but only opens in the high season, whilst the large, new Taverna Aposperitis, right beside the beach, offers cooked food in the evenings.

Vital Information

As there are no banks visitors should exchange money before arriving at Donoussa! The only recourse for those with no cash is the goodwill of the owner of the Blue Lagoon, who prefers German Marks to English pounds...

There isn't a 'proper' post office either, mail being sorted at the 'Koinotita' (village hall), which opens between 0800-1200hrs, as well as some evenings. This building, with a flagpole outside, is located a couple of streets back from the quayside, to the right of the big blue and white church. Stamps can be purchased, and it serves as a *poste restante*. The office is a veritable Aladdin's Cave of Greek paraphernalia, piled high with dusty papers, maps (not useful ones) photographs, stamp pictures, and topped off by a broken bouzouki balanced on the heap..., all of which helps to inspire great confidence in the fate of one's postcards!

The doctor is located in the same white building and his clinic is open weekdays between 0700-1300hrs, and 1800-1900hrs. The dispensary doubles as a pharmacy, and even as a surgery for the dentist who visits the island sporadically. (Get your teeth fixed before you arrive...). There is a surprisingly modern and efficient looking OTE office, but   getting a telephone line is another matter... It opens weekdays from   0900-1200hrs and 1800-2100hrs, Saturday between 0900-1100hrs and 1800-2000hrs, closing on Sundays.

Shopping requirements are catered for by two general stores. One is part of the Taverna To Kyma, where they sell island maps, as well as black and white line drawing postcards - the only available cards of the island. (That will not last long.) The other general store, along the port road just beyond the beach, is owned by an old man whom I found to be not only very bad tempered but who seems a little crazy. I patronized To Kyma - despite meeting a friendly mouse on top of the rice sacks...

The bakery seems too good to be true for such a small island, which it is, as the baker heads back to Athens at the end of the summer! The shop, which is only open between July and August, makes a fabulous selection of pastries. When the baker is not present, bread is shipped over from Naxos, weather and sea state willing!

Donoussa has no: roads, wheeled transport, ferry boat ticket office, police station, port police or disco. Hooray!

Beaches

The beach at the port village of Stavros is excellent: wide, sandy and quiet. Most islanders bathe here at some time during the day, and there are large notices forbidding camping and nudity, which should be observed (see Kendros beach as an alternative). A very little shade is provided by one or two tamarisk trees, but the location is   rather smelly and limited. The islanders use umbrellas to avoid the sun's rays.

Kendros Beach There are two routes to this fine, sandy beach, which is located just over the hill from Stavros. Both involve crossing the village beach and heading up the cement path leading to the church and beyond. This is the outset of the round-the-island donkey track which eventually leads to the next valley, from whence a dried up river-bed serves as a path to Kendros beach. A quicker route is to turn right just before the last house, going up the rise, the one surrounded by a low white wall. After which follow the faint path around the headland until it drops spectacularly down to the beach. Camping and nudism are permitted. This is an excellent bay, with clear, (cold) water, but no shade. For more beaches, see Excursions.

Excursions
There's only one excursion - a hike around the island. This trek is a major affair, and requires a couple of days' stay on Donoussa. The whole thing could be completed in one day, but you would have to set out early, very early in the morning, and be prepared to walk in the heat of the midday sun. I advise camping at **Kalotaritissa** and taking it fairly easy. Wear strong shoes to cope with the rocky paths, pack some supplies, purchase the island map (at the Taverna To Kyma), and check directions with the owner of the Blue Lagoon, bearing in mind he is very optimistic about timings. Water is available at Mersini.

This circular donkey path links Donoussa's settlements, leaving Stavros to the east, crosses the beach and climbs over a low-rise. The track then climbs out of a dry river valley, ascending steeply until it reaches **Mesaria** village, with its half-dozen inhabitants, about an hour's walk from the port. From here it is possible to descend to **Vathi Limenari** beach, which is mainly shingle, set in a narrow inlet, and good for snorkelling. Unless only walking as far as Mesaria, this beach is not worth the detour. From Mesaria the mountainous track continues to **Mersini** - another hour's walk away. A little more flourishing than Mesaria, Mersini has twenty or so villagers, and fresh water springs nearby. These promote pretty verdancy, and enable them to grow peaches, pomegranates and tomatoes. From here it is worth making the twenty minute detour down a path to the magnificent sandy beach at **Livadi**. The next stage of the hike is long and tough - north to Kalotaritissa. This small settlement sits beside the island's very best beaches - golden strips all around the bay, as well as a few palm trees to add to the glamour. You will probably decide to increase the current village population of seven people, and stay on forever! Depending on your walking speed, **Kalotaritissa** is between four and six hours away from Stavros, by the circuitous route. The 'short cut' back to Stavros is almost as long as the roundabout route, and it is easy to get lost....

Island Customs, Feasts, Specialities and History
Not many. Locals claim that the present-day population is descended from Amorgot farmers who migrated some two hundred years ago. Although Donoussa was inhabited in ancient times, pirates ruled for many centuries, and the island was only re-inhabited after their departure.

The island produces a sweet red wine, and also raki, a distillation of ouzo, more commonly linked with Crete.

A French social study   in the 1960s recorded a very backward and difficult lifestyle, with 56% of the population aged over forty five totally illiterate. This was probably true of many similar island communities, where, even today, many old people cannot read and write.   Incidentally this document, in French, is the only kind of tourist information the island authorities have to offer!

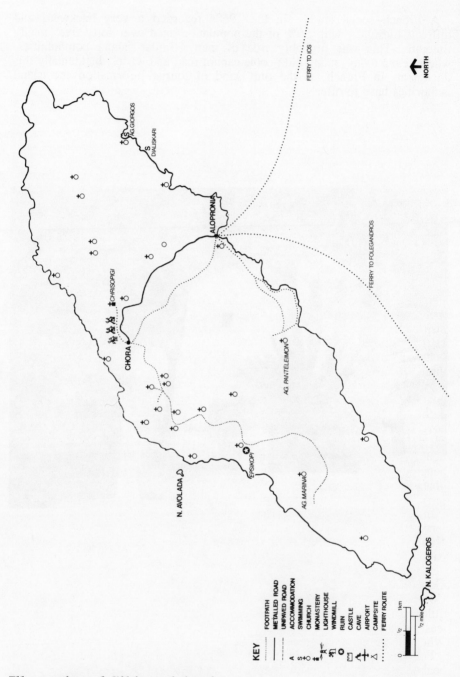

Illustration 6 Sikinos island

CHAPTER FOUR   SIKINOS

On a scale of 1 to 5: Appeal: 4 Exploitation: 2 Beaches: 3 Scenic Beauty: 3 Accommodation - standard: 3 Accommodation - availability: 4 Facilities: 2	Sites to visit: 3 Accessibility: 5 Population 300 Telephone prefix: 0286 Size: Approximately 14km from one end to the other, and 5km wide.

Location
Towards the southern end of the Cyclades group, some 30km north-west of Santorini, and only 8km west of Ios island.

Getting There
Airport: No, the nearest being on Santorini.

Ferries: Because Sikinos is so close to Santorini and Ios, and is situated 'between' the western and the central Cyclades, it benefits from a disproportionately frequent ferry service. In high season, at least one ferry calls every day - many Santorini ships stop on their way both to and from that island, which is just over an hour away. In winter, Sikinos still 'enjoys' three ferries a week.

Whatever the time of year, because there is no ferry-boat quay, a fishing boat has to meet the larger ferries in the bay. This makes a lovely sight at night, to those safely ashore, but is not so appealing close up, since the cove is poorly protected from the winds. At best, this arrangement means an 'exciting' transfer, which consists of being either lifted into the transport boat by a burly fisherman, or thrown out of it on to the ferry's tail-board, hanging in the air, more than a metre above the wildly rocking passage boat. In inclement weather, the north wind prevents any such antics and the ferry sails on by. Be sure to allow for possible hitches in any arrangements!

Incidentally, the fisherman/ferryman charges for the passage between ferry and shore, though he doesn't appear to charge the locals. I have observed tourists, successfully resisting payment, but I do not object to paying a handful of drachmae for the service.

General
Considering its proximity to 'Paradise' (otherwise known as Ios), lovely little Sikinos has remained amazingly untouched by tourism. This is due, at least in part, to its lack of a quay suitable for the large inter-island ferries. When this is eventually constructed, the place may well become overrun.

For the time being, strangers are few and far between, and outside of peak season you may well be one of only a dozen or so visitors on the entire island. For obvious reasons, the number of vehicles is negligible - one bus, two mopeds and a car at the last reckoning. Thus Sikinos retains all its tranquillity and pre-20th century atmosphere.

The islanders of course do not relish living in the last century, and are vociferously unanimous in their desire for a new ferry boat quay. The promise of this, and the provision of a school for children aged over twelve, some four years ago (it now has six pupils), helped   stem rampant depopulation. Despite which, locals shake their heads and say that such improvements have been too late in coming - most people have already left.

There are two - well, strictly three - villages on the island: the port, and the Chora. The latter actually consists of two settlements, one to the left of the big bus and mule terminus square, the Chora 'proper', and one to the right named Kastro. These facts are as related by an islander, but other authorities differ on which settlement is which! In the winter the port is all but deserted, as everyone moves back up the mountain to the Chora.

Cycladically dry, without appearing painfully barren, Sikinos has a fine sandy beach, a friendly population, a pretty white Chora and a few excellent hikes - what more could you ask?

Incidentally, despite the tens of thousands of tourists who descend on Santorini every week, that spectacular island is a 'must' for every visitor to the Aegean. It is like no other island, Greek or otherwise, that you have ever seen. There are a few trip boats from Santorini to Sikinos, in peak season, but only a sparse number of private yachts call in at this poorly sheltered harbour.

Accommodation

There are plenty of rooms for the visitor who avoids peak season by a few days, either way: arrive on August 1st and you   may find all the rooms taken; by the 20th Sikinos is practically deserted. If the accommodation in the port is full, catch the bus which meets the ferries, and head for the Chora, where there are several pleasant pensions.

Alopronia (The port) A cluster of buildings with rooms are situated close to the jetty, where the fishing boat unloads its cargo of humans and goods. Room owners often meet the boats, but if they don't, proceed down the quay, beyond the village square (where the bus waits), and turn left. Three accommodation blocks sit side by side; Loucas Rooms are less expensive than the Pension Kountouris, which is run by a rather lecherous old man and his 'dragon' of a wife. They also own the taverna and the ferry ticket office beneath the pension - all of which are entered from the rear.

Loucas Rooms are simple, small and clean, with stone floors, a washbasin in the room, and a cubicle-like private bathroom down the hallway. Each room is assigned a bathroom, though you may need to sneak into your neighbour's, as the showers are temperamental and the water pressure extremely low. There's no hot water either, but despite the disadvantages, this is a good deal, especially taking   into account the balcony and excellent view over the beach. Next door is another block, Rooms Flora (tel 51214).

The Loucas family seem to be island property tycoons - they own other rooms in Alopronia, on the opposite side of the bay, above their taverna.

This building, which is marvellously situated and juts out over the sea, may be a better option still than the 'square-side' rooms, and certainly is quieter in high season. There are two more pensions beyond this taverna, on the headland, but they are only open in peak season.

Back by the quay, a concrete path takes off to the left out of the bus-square, leading to two houses with rooms, on top of the rise. These have marvellous views across the water to Santorini.

The Chora For convenience's sake, 'Chora' refers to both hilltop settlements. There is a fair amount of accommodation which includes yet another Loucas, block as well as the pleasant Pension Nikos above the Kafenion which sits on the main street of the right-hand settlement (heading towards the monastery/windmills).

Nikos' modern rooms cost more per night than Loucas, down below, but they are still reasonably priced, and include en suite bathrooms and hot water. Incidentally, Nikos is the father of the bus driver, and was partly responsible for bringing the bus to Sikinos, in 1988, hence its photo being on display in the Kafe. Nikos is friendly and helpful to tourists, beyond the call of duty, and totally reliable. His English is limited, but with the cafe custom there is usually someone around to help out.

Camping The island has no official site and camping on the port beach or in the field behind is not encouraged. It does occur, mainly because there are very few unobtrusive locations around - it is rather a trek to Agios Panteleimon beach, added to which there aren't any supplies there.

Food and Drink
The choice of dishes, outside of peak season, is severely limited. The lack of fresh, varied food is blamed on the lack of a ferry boat quay (as are most problems), because the supply lorries which serve other islands, cannot drive on and off here.

In Alopronia, Snack Bar To Meltemi, at the end of the quay, serves some food: little fried fishes, meatballs, salads and omelettes - standard Sikinos fare. There is also the aforementioned Taverna Kountouris, which is easy to miss because it has no outside tables, and is entered from the rear, and occupies the ground floor of the like-named Pension. The food here is a little more diverse than elsewhere, and includes fresh fruit, as the owner 'triples' as a greengrocer and general store keeper. Single women may feel uneasy under the direct observance of Panayiotis, and the hard stare of his no doubt long-suffering wife.

Across the beach, Loucas Rooms houses a taverna over the sea. Prices are low but the choice is limited: only meatballs or spaghetti, and no soft drinks or ice cream either!

No doubt these tavernas offer a wider range of fare in mid-August than in early September. This is certainly the case in the Chora, at the very pleasant Taverna Ta Klimataria ('The Vines') which includes on its 'excitingly' long menu 'ollish variety' and 'cakes spoon'. However, few of the promised dishes are available in September. To quote the owner, "finito la fiesta".

Despite the creakingly slow service, which requires many reminders, the pizzas are good and the taverna is the hub of Sikinot nightlife for the under fifties. Backgammon boards and packs of cards are readily available, and this is really the only source of evening entertainment on the island!

Just around the corner from Ta Klimataria is the previously referred to pleasant Kafe owned by Nikos, where the over-fifties gather for their evening's recreation. On the same street is the Taverna Ta Kaminia, which is only open during the height of season.

Vital Information

There is no bank on Sikinos. Mr Kountouris - he of the pension, taverna, general store and ticket office - dabbles in exchange, at the port. The official place to change money is at the Chora post office which is open weekdays between 0800-1430hrs. The office doubles as an OTE and there is also a coin telephone outside. Take the bus to its first stop at the Chora, and the post office is just along the road, on the right. Alopronia has a metered telephone in the small cafe on the square, beneath Loucas Rooms.

Most other facilities are in the Chora and the bus, which is 'based' there, rather than in the port, meets the ferries and makes the fifteen minute journey about seven times a day. It parks near the wide square, in between the two hilltop villages. The road beyond this square - the scene of a great deal of donkey work in the mornings, as water is hauled into the villages from the communal well - is apparently being widened still further. Maybe this is so the bus can toil even higher!

The 'left-hand' Chora village conceals the police station, on the left of the main street and recognizable by its flagpole. It looks deserted and actually has a "For Sale" sign on the wall, despite which the policeman is smiling and pleasant. There is no separate port police, at least not yet. The doctor is also based in the Chora (near the bus pull up), that is when he is 'in' - he sometimes 'goes away'. But then Nikos claims they have no need of a doctor, "everyone here lives to be over eighty". To support his declaration he indicates a couple of post-centenarian examples including that of "One woman who was ninety, went to the doctor with a headache and he told her to take an aspirin. But she didn't know what an aspirin was!" Let's hope the healthy atmosphere also affects visitors, otherwise it's just too bad!

Shopping involves venturing into the depths of a few Chora based general stores, where there is also a baker. The latter slaves away in a tiny house, near Ta Klimataria taverna, baking the island's bread in a vast wood-fired oven, which is worth seeing. The baker 'rents out' his oven to the rest of the Chora's population, and a steady procession of women bearing cooking pots and casseroles can be observed leaving his shop around lunchtime.

Down below, at the port, a Kafe/general store on the square, sells whatever commodities are available. There are no tourist shops (hooray) but maps and postcards can be purchased from Mr Kountouris. He also sells. ferry boat tickets, and a list of ferry boat times are displayed on the wall of his taverna.

Despite the island's serenity, it does support a disco, located a short way up the Chora road from the port, and safely out of harm's way. This is only open mid-season.

Beaches
Well, those staying in Alopronia have the best beach on the island right outside their front door. This long and sandy beach is backed by fields and an almost dried up river-bed. Perhaps the only drawback is low-flying sand during the frequent windy periods.

Agios Panteleimon This pretty, pebble beach is accessible by a scenic hike north from Alopronia but, in high season, you can cheat by taking a fishing boat in both directions. Two different fishermen offer trips from the quay, though the boats do not sail every day.

To walk takes about forty minutes. Follow the concrete path, which takes off left from of the post-box/bus terminus square, past the Rooms, and continue along beyond the smattering of new villas which are being constructed, with views across to Santorini. The path is clear for a distance, until it reaches the bottom of the first valley, and begins to rise, following the dry river-bed. Here you have two options - either to climb on upwards (the path becomes distinct where the rocks end - hug the wall) or to strike out left and follow a goat path right around the coastline.

Those selecting the second choice and heading for the sea, should follow a very narrow, almost indiscernible path which leads below some tumbledown farm buildings, around the end of a promontory and behind a new house. This area is known as **Tria Pighadia** (three wells). The narrow path continues round the inside of a small bay - climb down the terraces, following the goat droppings, and scramble up the other side. Despite the difficulty of following any path, if you simply stick close to the coast (avoiding the occasional rocky cleft...) you will eventually round the final headland, where the chapel of Agios Panteleimon becomes visible at the end of the valley. To reach the beach necessitates a climb down a low cliff.

The beach is worth the effort, being quiet, with many rocks from which to jump from into the sea. Additionally, there is the attractive and useful feature of a cave, by the sea's edge, which provides shade and atmosphere! To return by the other route, strike off up the right-hand side of the valley (sea behind one). Unfortunately the path hereabouts is practically non-existent. However, just beyond the point opposite the chapel, the main path crosses 'your' goat track: turn right up the steeply stepped hillside, from whereon the path back is wide and straightforward.

Agios Giorgos and Dialiskari These beaches, north of the port, are only accessible by boat or a tremendously long and difficult hike, from the Chora, along mule and goat paths. In high season caiques run to and from these sand and pebble beaches almost daily, leaving at around 1100hrs and returning at around 1600hrs. There are no facilities or shade at either beach, so be sure to take along all supplies.

Agios Leftheros The only beach to which the Chora can lay claim is reached along a path from the main square between the two parts. Some thirty minutes down the track leads to flat rocks and an impressive view, but not a very sheltered bathing site!

Sites to See

Chrisopigi Monastery Standing above Kastro (the 'right-hand' Chora settlement), the Chrisopigi Monastery/Kastro was originally constructed in the 14th century, apparently on the site of an ancient temple to Apollo. It is undergoing fond restoration at the hands of the islanders. To get the key, ask at Nikos' Kafe - he will direct enquirers to the family which holds responsibility for the village's churches, one of whom will accompany you to the monastery.

The path passes ruined windmills and affords spectacular views over towards Folegandros. The flowered courtyard and church of **Zoodochos Pigi** are pretty, the scenery is even more impressive, and the guide is only too willing to show you one of the cells which has now been restored and lovingly converted into a mini-museum. It contains a fireplace scene with old-fashioned furnishings, as well as various relics from the island. The *piece de resistance* is the old door to the monastery, behind which the islanders took refuge on occasions, from pirate invasions. The holes in the door are said to have been made by the pirates' bullets.

The Temple of Apollo This is a fascinating ruin: small, but quite outstanding in its preservation. The temple, now known as **Episkopi**, can be reached either on foot from the Chora (a 4km trek) or by mule. Mules can be hired from Nikos Margetis, he of the aforementioned kafe, and it is necessary to take him along as an escort, unless you happen to be an expert mule handler! This may seem an expensive alternative, but it lasts three hours and includes a personal tour guide - the ride takes roughly one and a quarter hours, each way. It is an experience you are unlikely to encounter on any other Greek island... the sort of thing travel writers in Greece were describing about forty years ago. The monument is well worth the trip - those who travelled by mule will surely think this is an end in itself.

The mule path hugs the steep side of the mountain, travelling parallel to the island's north-east coast, with spectacular views towards Paros, Sifnos and Folegandros. At first passing many cultivated fields, thick with vines, the track continues above flat farming plains down by the sea, many of which are still terraced but have now run to seed. The hovels in the fields used to be homes and, according to Nikos, entire families were raised in these isolated homesteads, mothers using an upturned donkey saddle as a cradle for their infants.

The temple, popularly believed to be in honour of Apollo, may have been constructed around 2000 BC. An inscription found nearby refers to Apollo Pythios... less romantic theories suggest that the structure was actually the family tomb of a wealthy Sikinot family. The crypt below, which can be visited, using a torch, contains a number of graves.

Around the 5th century AD the building was incorporated into a religious structure, later destroyed. The present Christian chapel surrounding the structure was added in 1688, and dedicated to Episkopi (the Virgin Mary), which accounts for its present day name.

The conversion process resulted in one of the most peculiar monuments ever: the 'temple's' original massive pillars guarding the doorway, and its pointed roof and great projecting cornerstones in striking contrast to the curves and domes of the chapel in its midst. Such a solid example of forging old and new religions is rare indeed!

In the stone courtyard outside are two wells. Up to about twenty years ago, the islanders made an annual pilgrimage to the church, on its feast day of August 15th, but the tradition has been discontinued. From the temple, it is possible to continue walking across the surrounding terraced fields to the church of Agia Marina, which was used as a prison by the Italians, during World War II, and beyond which are very scant remains of an ancient city.

Excursions
See Beaches.

Island Customs, Feasts, Specialities and History
Religious Festivals The fiesta of Zoodochos Pigi is celebrated each year at the monastery above Kastro, on the Friday after Easter.

Island specialities include a soft, tangy cheese called *xinogalo* (sour milk), which is delicious but difficult to obtain.

In ancient times the island was known as Oinoe - island of much wine. Vines grow in abundance, but the wine is made at home and not available in shops, though Mr Kountouris has a dubious looking/tasting 'open' retsina for sale in his taverna. Other island products include honey and olive oil. Pastelli is an island speciality produced for weddings and feast days.

History Very little is known about the history of Sikinos, although it has been settled since ancient times, when the god Apollo was widely worshipped. The Romans sent exiles here, and later the Venetians became rulers, followed by the Turks. It seems that Sikinos has been sparsely populated for much of its history, as it is today.

PART THREE
The Dodecanese

Neither the glamour of the Cyclades, nor the green glory of the Ionian can overshadow the attractions of the Dodecanese island group.

While popular island destinations, like Rhodes and Kos, attract most of the crowds, the Dodecanese, many of which lie within a stone's throw of the Turkish mainland, also lay claim to a concentration of unspoiled islands. They are picturesque, less barren than the Cyclades, relatively easy to reach, and inhabited by wonderfully friendly people. Travelling this chain, you will doubtless come across a passenger ferry which visits almost every inhabited rock in these waters. Over the last twenty years this has been the good ship Panormitis, a rough, tough, small, slow and a somewhat battered looking boat. With the same captain at its helm. The FB Panormitis has ploughed the same route, a lifeline for remote islanders, summer and winter alike.

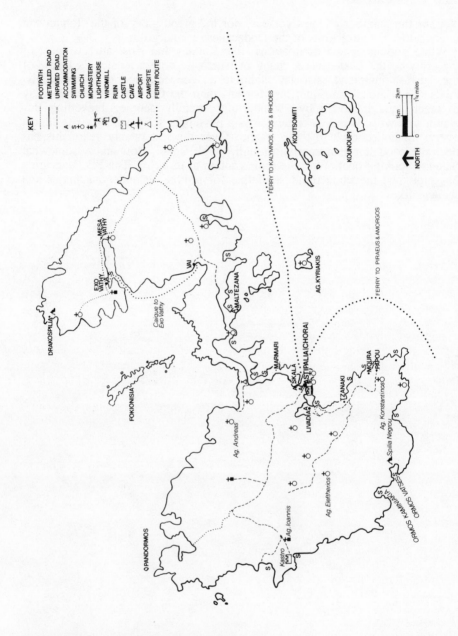

Illustration 7 Astipalia island

CHAPTER FIVE   ASTIPALIA

On a Scale of 1 To 5:	Sites to visit: 3
Appeal: 3	Accessibility: 4
Exploitation: 3	
Beaches: 2	Population: 1,100
Scenic beauty: 3	Telephone prefix: 0242
Accommodation - standard: 4	Size: Width at the broadest point
Accommodation - availability: 4	is 18km, whilst the greatest depth
Facilities: 4	is 14km.

Location
Sited in between the Cyclades and Dodecanese island chains, Astipalia is around 70km north-east of Santorini and 40km south-east of Ios.

Getting There
Airport: No (not yet, in spite of what the island maps show).

Ferries: Although Astipalia receives its fair share of ferries, timetables are annoyingly scheduled. Four days a week, most boats head towards Piraeus - and then for three days they steam to Kalimnos! In the main, ships from Piraeus arrive in the early hours.

General
Although Astipalia belongs to the Dodecanese, its nature is essentially Cycladic. The island's best feature is its glorious, Cycladean style Chora. This cascades down the barren Venetian castle capped mountain, over-looking and guarding Skala, the port.

The Chora's streets are a paradise for photographers, and the old town is in surprisingly sound condition. This is due, in part, to numerous foreigners who have purchased and renovated property, most locals having moved to the more practical location of Skala.

The natural beauty of Astipalia - which is shaped like a giant butterfly - lies in its great mountains, falling away to the clear blue seas. It is a wild, comfortless landscape, burnt dry brown; stark and inhospitable. A glimpse of the Chora, which can be seen from many remote areas, is reassuring.

Because it is a large island, Astipalia absorbs tourists well, and, even in peak season, is not overcrowded. Prices are low, the people are friendly and welcoming - this is a great place to witness unadulterated Greek island life. With so much to recommend Astipalia, it is a shame that the beaches are disappointingly narrow and scrubby. Some freak of nature has resulted in the island being completely free of snakes.

Accommodation
Rooms can usually be located, even in high season, and several villages cater for tourists, who are mainly Greek.

Skala and The Chora

A number of small hotels and pensions, greatly varying in standard and price, cluster around the port where the Hotel Paradissos is well recommended. If staying in Skala, it is worth   remembering that motorcycles constantly roar up and down the hill to the Chora, so try to avoid a room overlooking this street.

Should the port be full, pension owners in Skala usually have at least one relative in the seaside resort of Livadia to consult, otherwise head for the Chora. Here, rooms in private houses can be sought, although few are advertised. Many natives, who live in Skala or Livadia during the summer, leave their winter homes in the Chora empty, and if you ask around, someone will usually 'produce' accommodation.

Livadia The richest vein of accommodation waits in Livadia, a short bus ride from Skala. This fertile village also has the island's best beach (which isn't saying much), is well provided with tavernas, as well as other tourist facilities. Accommodation is reasonably priced, even in the peak season.

The bus enters Livadia via a narrow back street, then turns left down a dried up river-bed to the seafront. On the back road, right opposite the bus stop, is the Pension Nikos, identifiable by the high blue and white wall and tall iron gates. It is set in an orchard of banana, orange and lemon trees. The balcony, which runs around the upper storey, is heavily scented by the fruit trees below. What more could you want, besides low prices, friendly, English (Australian) speaking proprietors, and clean (shared) bathrooms?

There are more pensions bordering the summer dry river, as well as the other streets which lead away at right angles to the beach - besides a few establishments on the seafront, which usually fill up first.

Camping The island's official campsite is some way from the 'swing' of things, not that there's really much swing to worry about... It is signposted from the port and the Chora, to the right, about 3km along the road to **Maltezana** village. The site has a small taverna, a food shop, washing facilities and plenty of shade.

Food and Drink

There is an abundant choice of places to eat in Skala or Livadia. The Chora has no tavernas but outlying Maltezana has a couple of tavernas.

The best bet in Skala is the Taverna To Akroyiali, sited on the edge of the beach, with its tables and chairs spread across the sand. It can't be beaten for location, value or standard of cuisine, though its nearest rival in the latter two respects is the family-run Restaurant Australia, directly behind the Akroyiali, across the road and raised above it. In both cases the atmosphere is extremely friendly, the service adequate, and the prices low. Alternatives include the Albatross on the street beside the beach - good for breakfast and their mezzedes, whilst for a pizza try the restaurant at the top of the hill, on the road out of town towards Maltezana.

Vital Information
Skala and Chora Facilities are divided between the villages. Most 'civic' offices are in the Chora, and the rest in Skala.
The island has no banks, but the post office exchanges money and cheques. It is situated in the Chora, on the left, at the top of the steep hill from Skala. At the port, the Hotel Paradissos changes money, as does the representative of the National Bank of Greece, beneath the Hotel Aegean.
' The OTE office is set apart from the post office, down in Skala, beneath the Hotel Paradissos. It is a rather disorganised affair (what a surprise), theoretically open until 1500hrs on weekdays, and on Saturday mornings. A metered telephone lurks in the basement shop to the front of the Hotel Paradissos. Incidentally, this store sells island maps, but not reliable ones. Better head for the tourist office, Gournas Tours, on the seafront, where they have a choice of two maps. The best quality map is pinned to the wall. It can be recognised by the square photographs on the outside - the ...'bad' map has circular photographs. (Both, of course, boast "new edition" on their covers - who ever saw a Greek island map which didn't?) The bad map was reportedly sketched by an islander whilst sitting in a cafe: it details countless, non-existent roads and omits routes which do exist, thus doing more harm than good. Both feature a non-existent airport!
Gournas Tours offers trips to nearby beaches and rocks (see Excursions). There are two or three ferry boat ticket offices in Skala, each handling differing shipping lines, typical of which is the Economou on the 'balcony' area, in front of the Hotel Paradissos. Ferry timetables are posted up outside. Another office, at the bottom of the road to the Chora, on the right, handles the sale of Olympic Airways' tickets.
The police and port police are situated in the rather derelict, Italian-built Municipal offices, near the bottom of the Chora road. Officials communicate with the public by shouting out of the window.
Shopping is not too difficult, there are a few pokey general stores both in the Chora and in Skala, and a bakery in Skala, close to the Hotel Paradissos. Stores advertise 'free tax drinks' - a reminder that you are in the customs-free Dodecanese after all! The pharmacy and doctor's clinic are in the Chora, just to the left of the windy square at the top of the Skala road. They are actually housed in the basement of the Town Hall, but open directly onto the main street, due to the steep incline. There is a dentist just beyond the last windmill at the other end of the row.
Transport between Skala and the Chora is by frequent bus service; there are taxis, and moped hire can be located in Skala, the Chora and Livadia, with no problem. Incidentally, moped hire only 'hit' Astipalia four years ago, and motorbikes are the undisputed kings of the road... that's progress. The petrol station is right at the top of the Skala/Chora road.   It opens sporadically for an hour or two at a time, but is definitely closed on Sundays, pump it when you can!

Livadia
Livadia is green plots, pensions and tavernas, and the bus arrives frequently from Skala and Chora. In the centre of the village are a kiosk with a

telephone, and a post-box, and at the beach end of the river-bed is a water tap with clean drinking water. Very few islanders live here in winter, which explains the lack of shops and other facilities.

Beaches
Not the most outstanding feature of Astipalia. Skala has an adequate but not particularly attractive beach; Livadia's is better, being reasonably sized, but of grey sand. From here, and Skala, boats visit the beach at **Agios Konstantinos**. This beach may be less populated, but is not superior in quality to that at Livadia.

A dirt track from Livadia also ends at Agios Konstantinos, passing *en route* the of beaches of **Tzanaki, Moura,** and **Papou**. The first of these has a small taverna and rooms. Although some maps show this route dropping down to each of the beaches, in fact, it remains high above the sea until descending alongside the small chapel at Ag Konstantinos.

This sand and pebble beach is pleasantly backed by shady trees, often has campers, nude bathing, as well as a great view across the water and up to the Chora.

From Skala, caiques motor, two or three times a week, to the distant beaches of **Vatses** (interestingly close to the Negrou Caves) and to **Kaminiakia**. Neither is outstanding for its beauty.

Marmari Heading north-east from Chora towards Maltezana, beyond the new generating station, the road passes a string of coves, named on the map as Marmari A, B, and C. These provide secluded bathing in very clean seas, although the beaches themselves are nothing to rave about.

Sites to See
The Castle Standing 130m above the sea, the castle occupies an excellent vantage point, overlooking harbours at Maltezana, Agios Andreas and Livadia, as well as the main port of Skala: it is ideally situated for defensive purposes... and from which to take photographs.

Built around 1240 by the Venetian family of Quirini, who ruled the island from 1207 to 1522, the structure originally contained the whole of the island's main town within its walls. Some four thousand people lived here at one period, although the average population over the years was around two thousand five hundred. Today it is possible to explore the ruins of houses, and see the two well maintained churches, one of which stands over the castle entrance.

The Quirini coat of arms is still visible above the gateway, which leads into a vaulted passageway where business and trading were carried out - the first building to the left of the entrance was a cafe. The town square stood before the church of Agios Giorgos, in the middle of the Kastro.

Most houses were three or four storeys tall, with one family living on each floor of a building. Sanitation problems were solved by a complex underground sewerage system of clay pipes, while drinking water came from cisterns. This, presumably proved effective as there are no records of any epidemics in the Kastro. One way of letting a more light and air into their crowded lives was for the inhabitants to open holes through the castle wall, and dozens of windows in the fortress are clearly visible from outside. By the beginning of the 18th century, the settlement began to expand beyond the castle walls in ever increasing circles, despite which, the people remained close enough to take refuge within the Kastro in times of danger. Eventually, eight different neighbourhoods were established in Chora, although they could hardly be distinguished by outsiders.   **Portaitissa** is the area around the castle gate. An old island song differentiates between the various settlements, and one line goes, "The beauties are in Kastro, the spoiled girls in Palos, and in the neighbourhood of Karai are the girls who marry young."!

The last inhabitants abandoned the Kastro in 1943, and building materials were taken for new homes outside. Further destruction was wrought by a big earthquake, in 1956.

The fort and upper part of the Chora were built on the site of an ancient acropolis and town. Some homes in the Chora contain marble blocks which were probably bits and pieces from the original ancient city.

Island Caves Astipalia has two large cave complexes, neither of which has been developed for tourists. The local people know where they are, and those determined to visit will be able to find a guide. Ask in Livadia for the Spilia Negrou, and in Exo Vathy for the Drakospilia.

Spilia Negrou: The 'Caves of the black' are located at Vatses bay, in the south-west corner of the island, and reach a depth of some 150m. These caverns were apparently named after a negro pirate who used them as a hideout, in antiquity, storing his treasure with the bodies of his victims...

Inside are stalactites and stalagmites, and many tunnels in which it is easy to lose one's way. When the caves were explored early this century, shepherds found a dome-shaped chamber, containing an altar, as well as some human skeletons. The caves are supposed to have been a refuge for Christians fleeing from the Romans.

Their modern-day moment of glory came when they were used as a hiding place for English resistance fighters, during World War II, as related by Michalis Palatianos, Astipalia's 'island guard'. Incidentally, island guards were a customary official on unpoliced islands, a civic appointment dating back fifty years. During the German occupation, five members of the British Resistance living in the Vatses region, and only the island guard, the teacher and a couple of other officials knew of their whereabouts. Rumours abounded, however, and the Germans decided to search the region, but the Greeks, using string as a guide, took the British deep into the caves and stayed with them while the machine-gun toting Germans roved the hillsides above. The caves have two separate entrances, a large and a small one - the Germans found the large one, but the cave behind is shallow, and they were unable to find the smaller entrance leading to the deep cave.

Drakospilia The 'Dragon Caves' situated near the northernmost tip of the island, not far from the tiny hamlet of Exo Vathy. They can be reached from there by sea, but only in extremely calm weather, as the waters around the cape are extremely dangerous. The turbulent seas are one clue to the caves' name - locals opine that the dragon sat at the entrance to his den, looking towards the dragoness who lived on Amorgos island. When he sighed, to bemoan the distance between them, the sea boiled and tossed furiously outside the cavern. Another story is that the first huge stalagmite near the cave's entrance is the dragon's throne, and a nearby stalactite resembles his cloak.

These stalactite hung grottoes, with matching stalagmites, are labyrinthine and have never been fully explored. To find them, ask at the taverna in Exo Vathy. A village shepherd, who daily visits a chapel near the entrance to the caves, to keep the candles alight, will take along interested parties. The goat path is otherwise almost impossible to follow.

Excursions

Agios Ioannis Monastery and Beach The monastery of Agios Ioannis stands at the top of a narrow valley on Astipalia's west coast, about 10km away from the Chora. The valley presents a surprising vista of fresh, green terraces which tumble down below the monastery, and a small house from which the farmer works the land. A path descends to the sea and a secluded beach, about thirty minutes' steep walk away. The monastery is locked.

Nearby are the 'invisible' remains of the Kastro Agios Ioannis, that is invisible from the beach and monastery, being only accessible to mountain goats. This castle was built in the 9th century, on a rock which is virtually unscalable. At one time, the islanders took refuge there from an attack by Turkish pirates. Unfortunately, an old lady, who remained outside, was forced to lead the way to the castle, with the result that the Turks broke in and slaughtered everybody in sight.

To reach Agios Ioannis: take the right turning from the Chora past the windmills, but instead of dropping down towards the port, turn left up the mountain - the road soon becomes unpaved. Ignoring side turnings, stay on this track, which affords views over Livadia's fertile valley, while climbing up the mountain towards an underground military base. The road divides just before the base, at a helicopter pad (marked H). The uphill fork leads to the base; stay on the other road, and keep left at the next fork. Remain on this main track all the way, ignoring a short path to the left, in the direction of a chapel. The countryside is painfully brown and barren, with a few scattered homesteads clinging grimly on to the barren landscape. You will observe a house and two fields with trees down below on your right, and soon afterwards reach a division in the road. Turn left on a track, which quickly leads down to the monastery, and may be indicated by a 'red Indian' style arrow made of pebbles, on the ground.

Agios Andreas Just before the isthmus, on the road to Maltezana, a left turn is marked "Agios Andreas Taverna in the wilderness". A dirt track progresses towards the north coast (incidentally, the sea to the north is the Aegean, to the south, the Cretan Sea). It skirts a wide bay, passing *en route* a massive, gravel grinding machine, terminating at a little jetty, and the shack-like fish taverna Agios Andreas.

The owner claims peace as the location's major attribute, but even that is shattered by the noise of the gravel diggings. The whole area is a wilderness, but not a very attractive wilderness. The taverna owner cooks fish at night, if he has any customers, which is not often the case. Occasionally ferries dock here in very rough weather.

Maltezana A dusty coastal settlement where the population of one hundred and forty are dedicated to agriculture and fishing. Maltezana, which took its name from an erstwhile community of Maltese settlers, has a few rooms, a couple of tavernas but no other concessions to tourists. Sadly the beach is not very appealing.

One site worth visiting lies at the entrance to the village, where a track behind the Taverna Obelisk leads to the remains of Roman baths, with well preserved mosaics. The owner of the taverna speaks English and directs enquirers along the short path.

There are about seven buses a day from the Chora.

Exo and Mesa Vathy The most remote settlements on Astipalia are the north-eastern 'Vathys', two hamlets with a combined year-round population of fifty or so. The road is passable as far as **Vai** beach, where it becomes more of a footpath than a road - access is difficult, even by moped.

A better way to reach Vathy is to take the caique which leaves Vai, mornings and evenings, throughout the summer. The Skala/Chora/ Maltezana bus connects twice daily with the caique service. This is operated by a family from Rhodes, who own a taverna at Exo Vathy and spend the summers here with their relatives, permanent residents of the settlement. The caique takes just twenty minutes to reach 'this' Vathy, Exo Vathy, where their taverna is the major feature. Nearby, a few dwellings squat among the farmland.

Exo Vathy is at one end of an almost landlocked sea inlet; Mesa Vathy is about forty five minutes' walk away, at the opposite end. The map marks a clear footpath between the two, but I have never been able to find it. The seaside goat path is interrupted by mounds of stones from a now disused granite mine. Mesa Vathy has no taverna and no accommodation, however, the Exo Vathy taverna has a few very basic rooms. Electricity is provided by a generator, which functions periodically, and water is drawn from a well. The young daughter, Dina, speaks some English, and this is the place to ask about possible forays to the Drakospilia (Dragon Caves), (See Sites to See).

The nearby beach is broad and sandy, and equipped with a structure offering shade, but because of its position at the end of the inlet, the water is not crystal clear. Still, it is a good place for children, being particularly shallow and warm.

Nearby Islets About three times a week, Gournas Tours, at Skala, offer scheduled trips, on fishing boats to **Agias Kiriaki** and **Koutsomiti**, two little islands to the south of Astipalia. These rocks are no longer inhabited, and have no particularly outstanding attractions of their own.

Island Customs, Feasts, Specialities and History
Religious Festivals Island feast days include: August 15th at Panagia

church, the Kastro; the festival of St John at Agios Ioannis monastery, on August 29th, and the chapel of Agios Konstantinos on May 21st.

Wedding Customs In the past, arranged marriages were the rule. After the matchmaking, the groom sent between twenty and one hundred golden Turkish florins to his fiancee, as an engagement gift. On the same evening, relatives and friends of the bride and groom visited the bride's house, carrying lights and bowls of sweets. The groom and his immediate family arrived last, when the groom's mother presented a pot of honey to the bride and kissed her.

As the groom entered the house, he was given a teaspoon of honey, after which he broke open a pomegranate onto the floor, which signified that the house should be full of all good things. The mother of the bride then presented the groom with the engagement ring.

The actual wedding ceremony took place either in church or at home, and involved the exchanging of rings and laurel crowns. Subsequently, the priest offered the couple a teaspoon of honey and almonds, then the local sweet-cake, serbeti, and pastelli, succeeded by a big feast, with much singing and dancing.

The marriage of a girl in Astipalia was an important event, and on her wedding day the eldest daughter automatically received the parental home, all the necessary furnishings and the mother's property as her dowry. This tradition of female inheritance was common on several other Dodecanese islands. In principle, the parents then had to leave the house, and were committed to providing a house for each of their other daughters as well!

Costume and Handicrafts Traditional Astipalian costume is one of the most eccentric and detailed of all Greek island dresses, and very different from any other Dodecanese garb. Its major features are a tall headdress draped with flowing, brightly coloured material, and broad sweeping sleeves covered by rich embroidery in the *skolopendrato* pattern of flowers and squares. The bodice was trimmed with fur, and wealthier members of the community decorated the costume with gold and jewels, fastening it with a silver belt. Sadly this costume is no longer worn.

Houses The original homes consisted of one long, narrow room facing on to the street. When building began, a priest was summoned to bless the first corner-stone, and crosses were placed at all four corners of the house, to prevent evil spirits from entering. Then an animal was slaughtered and its blood allowed to stay within the house walls. The builders ate the meat as part of the building festivities.

In the completed structure, the fire stood in the corner nearest to the door, beside the kitchen area. Recesses were carved into the walls as cupboards, but the most precious china and plates were stored at the opposite end of the room, on decorated wooden plate racks fixed to the wall. Next to these racks was the bed, at a considerable height from the floor, and screened off by lace curtains. A series of three steps, two of them wooden storage chests, had to be mounted to reach the bed, beneath which was a storeroom where the wine, oil and food stocks were kept. The

children slept in a partitioned chamber, beside their parents.
As the residents moved outside the castle walls, they gained space, and
were able to   create wider fronted homes. Distinctive features included
external wooden balconies, on which were mounted curious little wooden
huts called *poundia*, which enclosed the lavatory!

Folklore Local wisdom is often directed towards the fact that the island is
mysteriously free from snakes; indeed other reptiles such as lizards are also
scarce. No-one has ever provided a satisfactory explanation - scientific or
otherwise - for this unique (Greek) phenomenon. Naturally, legend claims
that St Anthimos, an island saint, cursed Astipalia's snakes, and there have
been none present since. An alternative theory attributes their absence to the
storks that fly over the island on their way to Africa, and yet another
suggestion is that there is some kind of mineral in the island's soil which
repels or poisons them. Islanders recount that a snake was brought here
during the last war, and released onto the shore, where, after a few minutes,
it 'burst'. Take your pick...

History Although the name Astipalia translates as 'old city', it is   also
attributed to the mythical goddess, Astipalia. She was the daughter of
Phoenix and Perimede, sister to Europe, and mother of Anceus, ancient
king of Samos, and Eurypylos, king of Kos, whose father was Podseidon.
Astipalia features in ancient Greek myth due to its disgraced Olympian
competitor, Kleomedes. This one-time hero killed an opponent during a
wrestling contest in the 71st Olympiad, subsequently he was stripped of his
laurels and went back to Astipalia, under a cloud of shame. Unfortunately
he chose to vent his frustration on the local schoolhouse, pulling down the
supporting columns in Samson-like fashion, killing the sixty or so children
inside. When the islanders sought revenge, the athlete was hidden by the
gods, and advice from the Delphic oracle informed them that Kleomedes
had been immortalised. Such is life!
The island was an outpost of the Cretan Minoan empire. In ancient times
it was named "Trapeza Theon" - table of the Gods - a tribute to its forests
and fertility, and clearly not a relevant epithet any more! Its other old name,
attributable to the Romans, was 'Ichthyoessa' or 'fishing grounds'.
In more recent history, Astipalia fell under Venetian rule, in 1207, and
passed between them and the Turks for a few hundred years. The Venetian
family of Quirini established some kind of stability and built the castle,
after they had arrived in 1413. The island became part of the Ottoman
empire in 1566, and enjoyed many privileges because of its strategic
position in the Aegean. Perhaps because of this, Astipalia did not play a
major role in the 1821 Greek revolution.
It was the first of the Dodecanese islands to fall to the Italians, in 1911,
again because of its location. A relic of their reign are a few Italian
municipal buildings, constructed in the port, as was common throughout the
Dodecanese. This need to build prodigious civic monuments reached its
acme on islands such as Leros. Astipalia was returned to Greece in 1948, in
common with the rest of the Dodecanese.

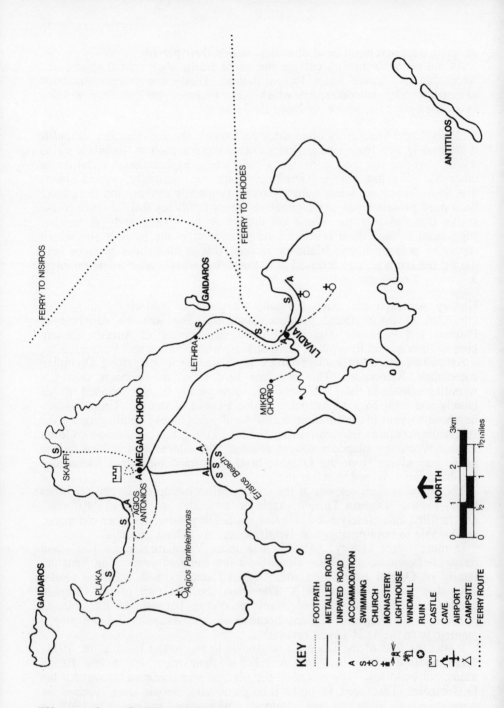

Illustration 8 Tilos island

KEY

	FOOTPATH
	METALLED ROAD
	UNPAVED ROAD
A	ACCOMMODATION
S	SWIMMING
+	CHURCH
	MONASTERY
	LIGHTHOUSE
	WINDMILL
⊓⊔	RUIN
	CASTLE
	CAVE
+	AIRPORT
△	CAMPSITE
⋯	FERRY ROUTE

NORTH

0   ½   1   2   3km
0   ½   1   ½ miles

GAIDAROS

FERRY TO NISIROS

FERRY TO RHODES

ANTITILOS

GAIDAROS

S SKAFFI

S PLAKA

A AGIOS ANTONIOS

A ● MEGALO CHORIO

⊓⊔

Agios Panteleimonas

A A S
Eristos Beach

S LETHRA

GAIDAROS

MIKRO CHORIO

LIVADIA
S A +

CHAPTER SIX   TILOS

On a scale of 1 to 5:	Sites to visit: 3
Appeal: 4	Accessibilty: 2
Exploitation: 3	
Beaches: 4	Population: 300
Scenic Beauty: 3	Telephone prefix: 0241
Accommodation - standard: 5	Size: Approximately 17km long,
Accommodation - availability: 4	and just 3km wide, at the
Facilities: 2	narrowest point.

Location
Approximately 65km due east of Rhodes, and 40km due south of Kos town, on Kos island.

Getting There
Airport: No, the nearest being on Kos).

Ferries: Tilos is not so simple to reach as its near neighbour Nisiros, because trip boats are few and far between, and travellers have to rely on scheduled ferries. A ferry boat calls twice weekly, in each direction, on its route between Rhodes and the more northerly islands. In addition, there are at least two other boats a week which link Tilos to the rest of the Dodecanese. The nearest 'hub island' ports of call are Kos and Rhodes.

Trip boats do call about once every two weeks and it is easy to recognise the signs of their impending arrival as this is a great village event, if for no other reason than the number of passengers on board can exceed the entire island population! When they dock, Livadia is flooded by waves of (usually Greek) visitors, who spill into the tavernas and then on to the beach, prior to departing within a few hours.

Using the trip boat to reach Rhodes from Tilos is not always a good idea. My own experiences once involved a boat, on which I was a passenger, calling *en route* at Panormitis monastery on Simi. Here it was overwhelmed by at least another one hundred tourists who had been left behind earlier that day, due to some administrative mistake. The captain refused to sail, claiming his vessel was overloaded. No-one would get off. The port police were called. Soldiers from the army camp wandered up. The passengers became more and more restless. Finally, the dispute only being settled when another boat was dispatched from Rhodes to assist. The vessel I was on eventually docked some six hours late, at 0100hrs, instead of 1900hrs!

General
Tilos is poor and isolated, and tourist development to date, has been minimal. Most visitors stay in the port, which only has an indigenous population of some fifty souls. This fact, encouraged by a lack of public transport, which keeps most people put, means that even a low number of

tourists become very obvious. Get out of the port Livadia, however, and you won't see another foreign face.

Tilos has two inhabited settlements, Livadia and Megalo Chorio. The pretty, friendly port and village of Livadia spreads beyond the ferry quay, interspersed by orchards, in amongst the branches of which perch the cicadas which make the place trill. A white pebble beach, shaded by tamarisk trees, stretches out along the bay for a couple of kilometres. Life is centred around the village square with its periptero and two cafes - local people are friendly, and a real bunch of characters. Some Greek is a great help, since few islanders speak English, but Italian is understood by many older folk. Whatever your language, the Tiliots are gracious and welcoming to all their guests.

Megalo Chorio, the Island's larger village, with a population of two hundred and fifty, is built on the site of ancient Tilos, well away from the coast. A paved road links it with Livadia but, at the time of writing, the total lack of public transport is the major obstacle which visitors must overcome. A bus is promised for the future... and will surely arrive soon. Fortunately, the island is excellent hiking country, with dozens of interesting destinations. The abundance of freshwater springs (which are marked on some maps) is a great bonus to walkers. This relative abundance of water allows sheep and goats to be grazed in the fertile valleys, for export to other, dryer islands, such as nearby Chalki.

Despite the ability to support crops, most foodstuffs, nowadays, are imported, as the small population cannot farm the land efficiently. The new bakery in Livadia at least does away with the need to import bread.

Accommodation
Livadia Until very recently the Hotel Livadia, on the village square, was the island's only hotel . Now there are several, as well as pensions, and plenty of private rooms not only at Livadia but elsewhere on the island. Prices in general are lower than average, but because of the lack of public transport, rooms in Livadia fill quickly, in mid-season. The Hotel Livadia's main competitor is the super-modern and 'painfully' classy Hotel Irini, situated outside the main village, along the beach.

While rooms at the E class Livadia are classically provincial, those at the Irini are indisputably de luxe; they have en suite bathrooms, and are sparklingly clean. With a swimming pool, telephone, and English book exchange, thrown in for good measure, as well as a jeep (at the guests' disposal, for a fee), it is not surprising that Tilos' few package tourists are safely ensconced at the comfortable Irini. Having justly sung its praises, I must add that the Irini's English-speaking owner might be considered unnecessarily pushy and flashy. He drives about in a car emblazoned with the hotel's name and is hell-bent on developing the tourist future of the island, with little apparent relish for its present tranquil state. Understandably he needs to earn his living, but his manner can be off-putting, despite his willingness to help every tourist who 'sniffs' the island's air. Rooms at the Irini are expensive; those at the Livadia are not.

Private rooms to be warmly recommended are Rooms Alex or Rooms Stamata. To reach these neighbouring seafront cottages, follow the road parallel to the sea-shore, beyond the square, where it passes behind a small orchard. Here, a paved track dips to the left, with "ROOMS" painted on the concrete, in gigantic letters. It leads only to these bungalows, which have connected patios built out over the pebble beach. The prices and conditions are identical, and the two old couples who own them seem to work in tandem, rather than in competition. Their rates are very low, and the establishments are spotlessly clean, with big refrigerators for the use of guests in the hallways. Both serve breakfast and other refreshments: sometimes they charge, sometimes they don't!

Livadia also has the Pension Castelli which is signposted from the village centre and is a little way back from the shore, behind a modern supermarket. It is clean, modern and inexpensive. Most rooms share bathrooms.

A few small bungalows for tourists, and built with public money, are strung out along the road, which runs parallel to the long beach. Most are block booked by a holiday company.

Megalo Chorio and the North-West Accommodation in Megalo Chorio is generally even less expensive than that in Livadia, but then the Rooms are not beside the sea!

Taking the road into the village, the first cafe on the left advertises cheap rooms which are spacious and pleasant, with clean, shared bathrooms. Other inexpensive rooms are scattered throughout the small town, although the rather out of place, purpose-built block of new rooms in the centre charges above average prices.

Beyond Megalo Chorio, the road divides. The left fork, still paved, leads to lovely **Eristos** beach, where rooms at the Taverna Tropicana are cheap and ideally situated, with shared bathrooms. A second taverna with rooms at Eristos is signposted, both from the main road (before it reaches Megalo Chorio, where a sandy track leads to the beach) and from the spot where the main road runs out on the beach. This latter taverna-complex is not a little odd, standing alone in the middle of nowhere, surrounded by low sand dunes and grasslands. The food is good, and the inexpensive accommodation is in little 'huts', linked by paths decorated with plastic toadstools. Perhaps the idea is to create a small 'oasis' in the sand. It is pleasant enough, but fly-infested.

Incidentally there are rumours of future hotels at Eristos and I'm not surprised, it's a marvellous location - so go there quickly.

Selecting the right fork behind Megalo Chorio, the road becomes unpaved but is well maintained. It leads to **Agios Antonios**, which used to have a beach but the sand was removed for building purposes - at least that is the claim of the owner of the Hotel Australia, which lies at the far right-hand end of the bay (facing the sea). This is a lovely hotel, very modern, with clean, spacious rooms... but why is it here? The hotel brochure claims it is "on the most beautiful coast of the island", which is nonsense. The hotel is usually empty (and therefore inexpensive), which is not surprising, because there is no beach to speak of, and the whole bay is rather wild and rugged - peaceful maybe, but certainly not one of Tilos' most attractive regions. The

hotel, which was built in 1986, has a small taverna.
The other place to stay on Tilos is the Monastery of Agios Panteleimonas (See Sites to See).

Camping Tilos has no official campsite but the far end of Livadia beach is a good spot, with trees for shade, and facilities nearby. Tents can be pitched on any of the island's more remote beaches, without local resistance.

Food and Drink
Most of the tavernas which cater for tourists are in Livadia. The best and the least expensive of these is certainly the Taverna Irina, a backslide establishment (near the big church) run by friendly, roguish Georgi, with tasty, well prepared food. Other places worth trying include the Taverna Blue Sky, on the ferry boat quay, which serves pizzas as well as traditional Greek fare. The owner, Yiannis, goes about with a severe expression, and a gruff manner, which is belied by the twinkle in his eye. He is a mine of local information, if he can be persuaded to spare a minute from his inexplicably hectic business to sit and talk.
Other offerings in the port include the souvlaki snackbar near the new supermarket, and the expensive Livadia Snackbar, in the basement of the Hotel Livadia. Across the street from the Livadia, the Fish Restaurant Trata is vastly overpriced and much too classy for Tilos.

Vital Information
Facilities for visitors are gradually expanding in Livadia, if nowhere else on the island.
The long, low building on the left of the main square (facing seawards) is the combined post office cum OTE office. Apart from making telephone calls, money can be exchanged, but the office is only open on weekdays, until 1400hrs. In an emergency, money can be changed at the Hotel Irini, but the owner prefers to reserve this service for his guests. Similarly, you can use the telephone at the Irini, but the rates are higher than at the post office. The telephone in the periptero only takes incoming calls, or at least that is the official explanation why tourists can't use it...
The police station (tel 53222) is the large, white building just off the ferry boat quay, on the Plateia Iroon Politechniou. This strange construction, which resembles an unfinished castle, houses one policeman and one customs officer, the latter also being employed as the port policeman.
The doctor's surgery (tel 53294) is on the first road to the right, beyond the big church of Agios Nikolaos, where the 'beach proper' starts. The doctor speaks English and Italian, and the clinic doubles as the village's pharmacy. There is another doctor in Megalo Chorio.
As already mentioned, public transport is one of Tilos' major problems, because there isn't any! There are no buses, no taxis, and neither is it possible to hire mopeds or scooters. This state of affairs is bound to resolve itself as the island's popularity grows, and surely it is only a matter time before moped hire, at the very least, is established. Until that time however, there are one or two possibilities.

Guests of the Hotel Irini can avail themselves of the establishment's jeep, but everyone else soon finds out about the island pick-up truck,   which 'parades' on the village square each morning, at about 1000hrs. This brown Datsun jeep ferries visitors wherever they would like to go - for a very reasonable fee.

The alternatives are to hitch a lift with another islander, (or to ask   him how to get somewhere... he will doubtless oblige) - or to walk...   There is no petrol station on the island.

Shopping must be either at the old-fashioned store on the square, or the new supermarket, beside the road beyond the square to the beach. Fresh food is only available after the ferry calls, but fresh fish can be purchased daily, from the fishermen who sit near the quay, selling off their catch.

Unfortunately, Tilos recently 'spawned' a disco, even if it is at a distance from Livadia, along the beach. How it survives is a mystery. Most tourists don't want one, and the locals never visit. In fact, it is almost always empty, except for a few soldiers from the tiny army billet, next to the church of Agios Nikolaos.

Beaches

The long, white pebble beach at Livadia is the most convenient, and is never crowded, despite its proximity to the village and tourist amenities.

The next nearest beach to Livadia is **Lethra** beach, a twenty five minute walk from the port. Although pleasant, Lethra is no more outstanding than Livadia's beach, but it is more secluded. To reach it, take the footpath, which begins as a road by the Hotel Livadia, and continue along the path, through a gate or two, across the hillside. The route follows the western shore of Livadia bay, rising until the island of Gaideros (or 'donkey') becomes visible. Around another bend, the path descends through a cultivated valley with fields and continues to the sea.

The island's very best beach is at **Eristos** bay on the west coast. It is a hike of several hours from Livadia, or about 3km from Megalo Chorio. Following the trans-island road beyond Megalo Chorio, select the left fork at the divide - this ends at the long, sandy, and deserted shore, backed by a few shady tamarisk trees, with a gentle incline into the water. Rooms are available nearby (see Accommodation).

Sites to See

The Church of Agios Nikolaos Admittedly there is nothing remarkable about this large church, sited outside Livadia, in the direction of the beach. However, it is pretty , and the ceiling is painted with stars. The priest, who spends a lot of time walking around the church, may well invite a caller in to look around. He explains seriously that the upstairs gallery is for the young, unmarried women, who must spend their time thinking of God, and not looking for husbands!

Mikro Chorio This ghost town is about 2km out of Livadia. Follow the steep, paved road which climbs the hill behind the port, in a series of hair-pin bends. As it levels out, after 1km, a narrow, cement road, marked

'OTE', takes off to the left. This actually leads up to the transmitter on the mountaintop, but after a hundred metres or so, you will observe a rough track between stone walls, on the right. A tiny, hand painted sign, at knee-level, indicates Mikro Chorio.

Even if you came this far on wheels, it is necessary to continue on foot, as the track is extremely rough. A ten to fifteen minute walk brings you to the centre of this sad, deserted village, last inhabited in the late 1940s. In keeping with the trend on many islands, the villagers abandoned Mikro Chorio to move to Livadia; much more convenient, and safe at last, from marauding pirates. The settlement simply became redundant.

Now only lizards, flies and jackdaws live on in the ruins - they are obvious everywhere, and keep an eye open for snakes. As you peer into the crumbling houses, look for the remnants of village life - great grinding stones, bread ovens and broken storage jars. At Mikro Chorio's highest point you'll find a tumbledown chapel, surrounded by barely covered grave pits. From here one can survey a valley with hundreds of disused terraces, guarded by collapsing windmills on the opposite hillside. They are re-minders of the time, not long ago, when Tilos was an arable, cultivated island. The story of Mikro Chorio and its abandoned farmlands is the story of every depopulated island in the Aegean, and, one fears for the future of many others.

The only building which is maintained in Mikro Chorio is the large church, painted in edible-looking pink, red and white. The key can be obtained from the cafe on the square in Livadia. In stark contrast to its surroundings, it is immaculately kept, both inside and out. The church is surrounded by a pebble mosaic courtyard, and over the gateway into the courtyard hangs a great bell. Each year, at the festival of Panagia on August 15th, the church's feast day is celebrated.

The Mastadon Caves Somewhere to the left, off the road between Livadia and Megalo Chorio, and beyond Mikro Chorio, lie the Harkadiou Caves where the bones of mastadons (small prehistoric elephants) were discovered in the 1970s. Considering that there is little else to boast about on Tilos, these bones have made an entry into every guide book which mentions the island. It is probably only a matter of time before someone sets up a 'Hotel Mastadon', or 'Taverna of the Prehistoric Elephants'! In fact, the bones were speedily removed from the island, and "nothing beside remains", as the poet says.

Tourists intent on seeking out the, now empty, cave receive lots of help from the islanders, as I have. In fact, I have never located the path, despite on one occasion the island heart-throb, from Livadia's cafe, sketching a detailed map. The distinctive landmark is a single cypress tree, visible on the left as you proceed along the road towards Megalo Chorio, shortly beyond Mikro Chorio. The path apparently begins where the road crosses a small, summer dry stream - and indeed I did find a path but it petered out after a few hundred metres. Unfortunately, a steep narrow valley separates the road from the hillside where the cypress marks the entrance to the caves, and it is not easy to cross without a path....

Megalo Chorio Dominated by a towering rock, bearing a Byzantine fortress, Tilos' biggest village is a good base for exploring the western side of the island, though it is about 3km from the sea. Megalo Chorio is visible from the road up to the right, and you must turn off the trans-island route, into the village. The narrow streets twist up between the houses in a veritable maze, and, if you can find them, there is a doctor's surgery, a couple of supermarkets, a post office, and a very pretty, large church. This may be locked, but it is possible to get the key from the administrative offices which surround the courtyard.

The Fortress An extremely steep path leads up from Megalo Chorio to the ruined fortress on top of the rock. Although forbidding, the climb only takes about twenty minutes. Leave the village on the path to the right, past the supermarket, which then bends left beneath the water retaining device, clearly visible on the hillside. The fortress is worth the effort, if only for the magnificent view over most of the island. This is the site of an ancient acropolis, and some parts of the walls can still be seen. Most of the ruins, which include a well-preserved gateway, are of the castle of Agios Stefanos. This was constructed by the Knights of St John, from Rhodes, when they ruled the island in the 14th and 15th centuries. The shell of a small chapel, decorated with 16th century frescos, remains intact inside the walls, and is worth seeing.

The Monastery of Agios Panteleimonas This monastery, in a truly spec-tacular location, is 'fitted out' with beds, blankets, and even a telephone for anyone who wishes to stay - in the style of the Greece of old, it's still free.

Getting to the place is the problem. The brown Datsun truck makes the occasional sally up there, and so does the Hotel Irini's jeep: open the monastery's visitors' book and you will see Hotel Irini scrawled in very large letters on almost every page...

Anyone hiking, or travelling under their own 'steam' must first ask for the key, at the first large house on the right of the road into Megalo Chorio. If no one is in, try the DEH electricity generating station, just outside the town - someone there should be able to help. Take the trans-island road beyond Megalo Chorio, forking right where it divides. The track leads to the wild, scrubby bay of Agios Antonios, at the right of which is the aforementioned Hotel Australia. There are traces of a former settlement in the shape of ruined cottages and tiny chapels. Turn left, away from the hotel, past a ruined windmill, and carry on around the headland.

The road continues past a track, which turns off into the low bay of **Plaka**, where there is fresh water and a few ruined cottages. It then begins a steep ascent, and the surface deteriorates into shale and shingle. You may well observe a bulldozer, as the road is remade each summer, prior to the feast of Agios Panteleimonas on August 27th. Anyone on wheels should take great care, as the road is very rough, and there is a steep drop to the sea, on the right.

Eventually you round the final bend to see the iron gate of the peaceful hideaway ahead. It is closed with a simple wire fastening, and inside the outer entrance lies an external dining and cooking area, complete with stone tables, benches, and cooking facilities. Open water storage tanks are replenished from a mountain spring and water flows through them constantly, but watch for snakes.

The monastery was built around 1703, by a monk named Laurentios. The inner courtyard is reached by continuing through the dining area, and up a flight of steps at the far end, past a primeval toilet block. On the other side of a locked door is a pebble mosaic square surrounded by three tiers of cells, converted into primitive bedrooms. In the courtyard, the small, red-tiled chapel can be opened with the key, and has Byzantine frescos dating from 1776. The bell tower allegedly once housed a bell which could be heard as far away as Crete (some bell...). One attempt at a pirate raid was quashed when locals dropped beehives on the invaders from the tower top, but on a later occasion, pirates apparently broke in, and stole the bell.

The story behind the construction of the monastery at this particular spot once again involves a miraculous icon. This was found here, removed, and made its own way back, so persistently, that eventually the monks gave in, and built a chapel around the icon, rather than moving the icon to another chapel. The twist to this particular story is that no-one realised there was water present, until they began to build the chapel - so the icon knew best all along...

Excursions

Fishing boat trips are organised on an *ad hoc* basis to various beaches which are inaccessible by foot. To find out about these, inquire in the basement of the Hotel Livadia, or at the Taverna Blue Sky.

Island Customs, Feasts, Specialities and History

Religious Festivals Religious dates include August 15th, when the festival of Panagia is celebrated at Panagia church, in empty Mikro Chorio. A second festival of Panagia is held on August 23rd, at the uninhabited Panagia monastery on the hillside near Livadia. On the 27th August, many islanders travel specially to the monastery of Agios Panteleimonas, to celebrate that sanctuary's feast day.

Wedding Customs Tilos wedding traditions are still followed - though more in fun than earnest these days. The lack of young people means island weddings are rather few and far between. The marriage takes place on a Sunday. On the previous Friday the groom takes his clothes and belongings to the bride's home, to the accompaniment of the village musicians. On Saturday traditional foods, including loukoumades, are baked, and different pastries shaped and placed in a large basket. Honeyed cakes are blessed with the saying, "may your life be as sweet as this honey".

On Sunday morning, animals for the wedding feast are taken to the bride's home. After the church ceremony, the party continues throughout the night. At about 3am the local 'lads' embark on a 'chicken rustling' excursion, to gather the poultry for the following day's soup. This is followed by an early morning salute outside the nuptial bedroom, usually begun by the firing of a rifle.

Dancing continues throughout the following day, when, late in the afternoon and no doubt much the worse for wear, one of the men 'disguises' himself as the groom, wearing flowers in his hair. The pretender then visits the bride, who offers him a drink, after which he tries to grab her hand and 'steal' her. At this point, according to tradition, the real groom steps in and makes his claim. If he manages to hold on to her, even after three attempts at 'theft', the false groom must retreat. However, if he loses the tug of war, the two men are supposed to fight it out.

This marks the end of village festivities, but on the Tuesday following the wedding, all the relatives of the couple gather together for a family meal.

Costume Womens' traditional dress, now rare, includes wearing pointed hats and a flowing veil, heavy gold jewellery as well as a bright apron over a red, black and yellow skirt.

Other Traditions Easter celebrations include a local variation - besides the red dyeing of Easter eggs, the islanders colour candles red with dye from the roots of a local plant. The children are sent to collect the roots and custom warns them they will meet a black man, who will only let them pass if they kiss his backside. The 'black man' is, in fact, a large black stone called the "backside of the black".

History As the brochure for the Hotel Australia puts it, "Tilos, which in ancient times was called Episcopi, and before that Anthousa, and even long before that in the depths of ancient civilization, who knows how else, shows signs of life from the palaeolithic period, and human presence from the depths of prehistoric times". Couldn't have put it better myself!

A famous islander, in ancient times, was the poetess Irini, to whom a statue near the quay is dedicated. Although she lived to be only nineteen years old, her contemporary fame spread throughout all Greece, and her poems rank next to those of Sappho. She lived on Tilos in the 4th century BC, and the ancients named her the female Homer. Only three hundred lines of her poetry have been saved, the most famous of which is The Ilakati - "the spindle". Her poetic inclination was despised by her mother, who forced her to weave, knit, and do the worst of the housework.

The discovery of the mastadon bones added a little extra interest to the island's ancient history - the remains of these prehistoric elephants, which are believed to have become extinct around 4600 BC, were found in layers of limestone in the **Harkadiou** caves (see Sites to See).

The remainder of Tilos' history has no elephants and resembles that of most other islands in the Dodecanese. Settled around 1000 BC by the Dorians, the island was part of the Athenian maritime league in 479 BC. It went through a brief period of independence in the third and fourth centuries BC, minting its own coins, but in 42 BC fell under Roman rule. Little else is known of its history until the Knights of St John showed up in 1310, and ruled until the Turkish invasion of 1522. In common with the other Dodecanese islands, Tilos was ruled by the Italians, between 1912 and 1948, after which it was finally reunited with Greece.

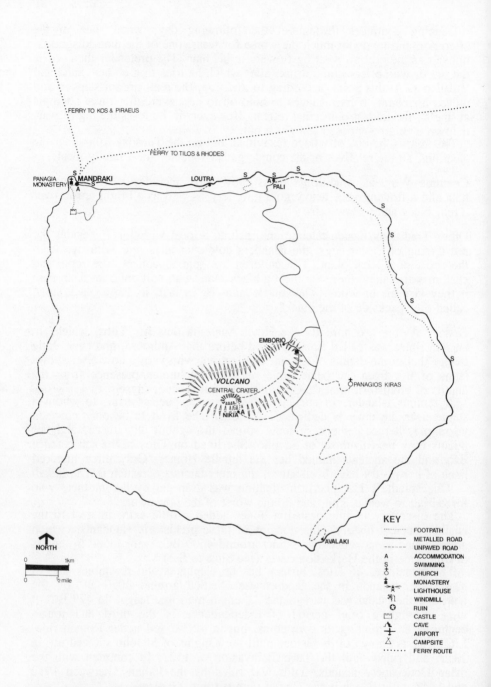

Illustration 9 Nisiros island

On a scale of 1 to 5:	Sites to visit: 4
Appeal: 5	Accessibility: 5
Exploitation: 3	
Beaches: 3	
Scenic Beauty: 5	Population: 1300
Accommodation - standard: 3	Telephone prefix: 0242
Accommodation - availability: 3	Size: Approximately 9km wide
Facilities: 4	and 8km long.

Location

Nisiros is 20km due south of the small port of Kardamena, on Kos island, and about 90km west of Rhodes. There are some 17km of sea between Nisiros and the Turkish mainland, to the east.

Getting There

Airport: No, but nearby Kos has one. Direct charter flights connect the UK to Kos in the summer months. Alternatively, it is possible to fly to and ferry from either Rhodes or Athens.

Ferries: In high season, trip boats travel six days a week from Kos port to Nisiros, a three hour journey (or shorter for those travelling from Kardamena). One scheduled ferry calls twice weekly, in both directions, and another provides a direct link between Nisiros and Piraeus, albeit a very slow and uncomfortable journey.

General

Nisiros is lovely, and unique: a dormant volcano, the only volcano in the Dodecanese - though not, as the island's tourist brochure claims "the only Valcano (*sic*) in Greece" - Santorini must have slipped their minds...

The volcano's presence explains the daily excursion boats from Kos: when tourists there tire of bars and beaches, a volcano makes an interesting alternative. Even so, more impressionable holidaymakers must find Nisiros a little disappointing - not because it is unattractive, but because the trip-boat owners advertise it in such lurid terms: "NISIROS - THE VOLCANO ISLAND" screams one chalkboard, decorated with drawings of red hot lava, flying boulders, and a gigantic mushroom cloud. One should point out that the volcano has not erupted for hundreds of years. Day trippers are bused up and down the mountain, and given a lightning tour of the port, after which they depart, leaving everyone blissfully at peace once again.

The fertile volcanic soil makes Nisiros beautifully green, compared to near neighbours such as popular Simi. Another peculiarity is that the island's economy is supported by the mining of pumice stone, especially on the offshore islet of Yiali. This industry employs most of the islanders, who thus do not need to rely on foreigners for a living, perhaps one reason why tourism is so under-developed, and the community so thriving. Still, despite the relative affluence, the population has dropped from four thousand, five hundred, at the beginning of the 20th century, to its present total of one thousand, three hundred. The most drastic effects of the exodus to Australia and the USA can be observed in the depopulated mountain villages of Emborio and Nikia.

The island's major settlement is Mandraki, with a population of eight hundred. The long, straggling village stretches along the seashore beyond the ferry quay. Its narrow, colourful streets weave in and out, like the patterns of a Greek dance, the weird tumbledown seafront looks as if it is crumbling into the sea, and there is an atmosphere of warmth and friendliness. Children play in the streets while their mothers either sit in the doorways, sewing or plaiting long strings of garlic, or wash clothes at the wells which appear to occupy almost every street corner.

Accommodation

Mandraki Most of the island's few hotels cluster around the end of the ferry boat quay, on the outskirts of Mandraki 'proper', this development has not intruded on the intimate character of the town.

The Three Brothers Restaurant & Hotel, and the Romantzo Motel are reasonably priced and comfortable; most rooms have en suite bathrooms. A little further down the road away from Mandraki, the large building labelled "hostel" is some kind of communally funded accommodation, only slightly less expensive than the hotels.

Following the street from the harbour into Mandraki, passes the expensive if very pleasant Rooms & Taverna Karava, on the right. Keep walking, and hope that Mama Anna, at the butcher's, still has vacant rooms. The sign outside her shop, (which is identified by a painted cow's head) says "Rooms to Rent". However the rooms are not here, but at the Pension Drosia, situated at the very end of Mandraki, almost at the foot of the vertical cliff-face, on which is superimposed a monastery. The two storey pension juts out over the sea, and each floor has a narrow, shared balcony where it is possible to dry washing and sit chatting, over a bottle or two... The large rooms share clean bathrooms and a kitchen with crockery, cooking equipment, as well as a fridge. The pension backs onto a tiny square, which is almost completely occupied by a large, central well. This square is a focus of street life, and women gather here almost daily, to use the well water for washing clothes. This pension has the distinction of being the cheapest I ever found, anywhere in the Greek islands. Other rooms are scattered throughout the village.

Pali This is a fishing hamlet, about 4km from Mandraki. The pleasant hotel near the sea, on the main square, is short on custom and thus charges very reasonable rates for pleasant rooms with en suite bathrooms. Other rooms at the two tavernas, and in private houses, are plentiful, and available at rock-bottom prices.

Emborio and Nikia There are no rooms in Emborio, (there are plenty of deserted, collapsing houses!) but in Nikia there is a community hostel.

Perched on the volcano rim, Nikia is a great place to stay, but accommodation is expensive, compared to Mandraki and Pali.

Camping Nisiros has no official campsite. Most people who camp do so on the **White Beach** near Pali (See Beaches).
The seaweed-strewn beach in Nisiros town is totally unsuitable for camping, and although the long, black volcanic beach at Pali is distant from the village, it is exposed and windy.

Food and Drink
Mandraki One or two of the hotels at the quay have tavernas and, considering the comparatively size of the settlement, there is an abundance of good eating places in Mandraki.
The Taverna Nisiros, in the village centre, does not enjoy seafront views, but it is an excellent establishment, well patronised by the islanders. Food is excellently prepared and inexpensive - even the fish is very reasonably priced. If the locals like the look of you, a complimentary bottle of wine may make its way to your table! Another recommendation is the superb Taverna Delfini which overlooks the sea. To search it out, continue beyond the main seafront square, towards the monastery, almost as far as the Pension Drosia. The taverna tables can be seen beneath a messy, thatched shelter, across the street from the low, little indoor kitchen which is decorated with pictures of dolphins. The old couple who run this establishment are friendly, the seafood is very cheap and they serve soumada, a rarely found drink made only on one or two Greek islands, from concentrated almond 'juice'. Dilute it with water and eat with dry bread or biscuits. It is very sweet, and non-alcoholic. After a few evenings patronage, various extra, free dishes may be thrown in...
Mandraki has numerous other tavernas - the Karava tends to be overpriced and rather 'mod', and there is also the peculiar Restaurant Spesial Franzis, edging the square beyond the Town Hall - this takes care of many trip boat tourists, and is more expensive than some establishments, though not criminally so. The chef-cum-owner is a very charismatic man with a vast jowl.

Pali, Emborio, Nikia
Pali has a couple of good, reasonably priced tavernas, one in the main village square, and another to the right of the square (facing seawards). Emborio has no tavernas, only a sad little cafe, but Nikia has one small establishment, near the bus station square, serving food as well as ice cream and cold drinks.

Vital Information
Nearly all facilities are concentrated in the port, Mandraki, which has a pleasant tourist information office. This opens daily at 1000hrs, when the boats arrive from Kos, and closes when they leave! They possess leaflets about the island, as well as ferry timetables and other useful information. The office is situated opposite the ferry boat quay, in a corner of the large square building. This also houses the Town Hall, the police (tel 31201) the port police, and the post office, where money can be changed.

A money changing office is run by a representative of the National Bank of Greece. To locate this, follow the road through Mandraki to beyond the liquor shop. This leads to the seafront square - the general store on the corner has a metered telephone, the best to use on the island, as long as you can put up with the store manager breathing down your neck! Continue along the road leading away from the seafront, and the 'bank' office is just beyond the fields, on the left.

Mandraki has both a resident doctor and a pharmacy. Mopeds can be hired from several outfits, including one bordering the 'general store square', or from the Romantzo Motel. Buses to the volcano leave from the ferry boat quay, about three times a day, before 1500hrs. Make sure you ask exactly where any particular bus is going, because some go right down into the crater, while others service the villages rimming the crater. One or two buses, on most days, proceed to Loutra, Pali, Emborio and Nikia, and the tourist office can supply details of the exact schedules. Compared to the otherwise generally low island prices, bus fares are high.

Ferry tickets are sold at the quay prior to a boat's arrival, by the very helpful, rather wizened little lady who runs a wholesale cigarette outlet/ Olympic Airways office which is located near the Town Hall, in the middle of Mandraki. Quite why Olympic operates a Nisiros office is a mystery, as there is no airport. On the other hand, the good woman managed to work wonders for me once when she recovered a lost rucksack forwarded to Spain, instead of Athens!

Shopping on Nisiros is not such a desperate affair as it is on many other islands - here at least they have their own bakery. This is in Pali, and the bread is brought to Mandraki by van and sold in several of the well-stocked general stores. Even such items as light bulbs and spark plugs can be purchased, but there is no petrol station, so those hiring a moped should bear in mind that the hire shop is the only 'source of power'.

Beaches
Mandraki There are only two beaches to speak of, and neither is very satisfactory. The village beach doubles as a children's playground, but is covered in seaweed, which is periodically shifted about by a rather unromantic bulldozer. I say shifted about because, as far as I have been able to ascertain, the activity seems totally meaningless, since the stuff is simply pushed around, to be finally dumped in a huge pile at one end of the beach. Perhaps it is periodically removed?

The alternative is **Koklaki** beach which is within walking distance and can be reached by following the path around the headland below the monastery. It is big, empty, unusual, and consists of large black pebbles. The tourist brochure describes these as "peculiar valcano stones" (*sic*) and they are uncomfortable for lying out on. The cave at the near end is occasionally used as a pigsty, which makes the area pretty smelly...

Pali Better beaches can be found by travelling the 4km to the nearby fishing hamlet of Pali. Just prior to the turning down to Pali, a steep, sandy track from the main road leads to the island's best beach, known as the 'White Beach', for obvious reasons. It is a broad sweep of fine white sand, the sort of 'holiday brochure ideal'. The water here is theoretically warm because of volcanic activity. Unfortunately, a massive hotel is under construction at the top of the cliff, which mars the scene. This de luxe effort, if and when completed, will be way and above the biggest and most modern hotel on the island, and may well draw increased numbers of tour companies to Nisiros. Fortunately, the developers are taking their time, and equally fortunately it is a comfortable distance from Mandraki, so the town may escape the worst affects of the resulting tourist 'deluge'. The White Beach can also be reached from Pali, by scrambling around the boulderous headland to the left of the harbour (facing the sea).

Stretching away to the right of Pali harbour is a long, volcanic beach of coarse black/brown sand. There is no shade, but a few rather decrepit beach umbrellas are to hand. A vast spa baths building is under construction at the far end of the shoreline. Following the road, which backs this long beach, passes the island bakery. Beyond the spa, the track becomes unpaved and very sandy, twisting over a small headland, before dropping down to the sea and the continuation of the volcanic beach. Watch out for snakes. The beach goes on for several kilometres, as does the track, to the right of which are orchards and pastures. Both end beside a rocky sea cliff where the shore widens out to form a wide, black, sandy cove. There are fruit trees all around, sometimes a few cattle grazing, and, just before the road ends, a small, ancient ruin with two short white marble columns lying about on the ground.

Sites to See
The Monastery of Panagia This monastery, dedicated to 'Mary, mother of Christ', perches on the cliff overlooking Mandraki. Originally founded in the 14th century, it is no longer inhabited by monks, but draws visitors to see its unusual chapel, built inside a cave in the rock. It can be reached by steps, signposted from Mandraki, at the opposite end of the town from the port. I am indebted to the island schoolteacher, Stavros Kentri, and his short book about Panagia monastery, for some tales of 'miraculous events'.

One story reports that, in the early nineteenth century, the infamous pirate Anastasakis went to the monastery, ostensibly to pray, but in reality he stole all the precious favours devoted to the Virgin Mary. However, when the brigand attempted to escape, he could not find the door, seeing only the stone walls around him. Not surprisingly he panicked, and a monk cried that Mary would not let him out with the stolen articles. When he replaced them, he was able to locate the door. Anastasakis was apparently so struck by the event that he later returned to dedicate a replica of a boat to the monastery.

The large number of silver goblets donated to the Panagia monastery also had miraculous origins. When monks entertained overnight visitors, during the evening meal they requested the guests to throw their glasses on to a rock 35 metres below the church. If the glass did not break, the guests had to donate a silver replica to Panagia. It is recorded that, "not only were the glasses unbroken, but sometimes even the wine did not spill"... It is not recorded how and by whom the glasses were collected and counted!

The Castle and Ancient Walls The Medieval Kastro was built around 1315 on the site of an ancient acropolis. It can be reached by ascending a further flight of steps from the monastery, or by wheeled transport from a road which sets   out near the port, passing behind the Romantzo Motel, and curving around the back of Mandraki, revealing lovely views over the town.
  The remains of the walls, dating back to the Classical period, are pretty impressive as they are constructed with huge blocks of black lava stone up to three metres thick in places. The fortifications formerly contained the whole settlement and within them, some remnants of the Medieval Kastro can still be observed. The surrounding fertile land is used for grazing cattle and donkeys, and the views are unusually lush and green for Greek island.

The Museum A small folk museum in Mandraki is furnished in traditional Nisiros style - there is a bed with a wooden storage box beneath, and the walls are hung with embroidery. The 'koskinas' and 'pardalaki' are island designs for hand-worked sheets. It was the custom to hang the green, red and black embroidered work on the wall, above the bed. The museum also exhibits island costume, which for women consisted of a red pinafore over a heavily embroidered tunic with bell shaped sleeves, and a headscarf. Nowadays this is only worn on rare occasions.

Loutra (Spa) This collection of vast stone buildings and water tanks, which on closer inspection proves to be spa baths, is some 2km from Mandraki. The waters of Nisiros are radioactive and therapeutic, and have been used for curative purposes for over one hundred years. Loutra, which resembles a rather frightening Victorian sanatorium (with lots of baths), is solely for the use of convalescents. Not only is there accommodation but a tumble-down taverna and a small chapel. Most writers state that the seas around Nisiros are hot. I cannot say I have ever noticed this phenomenon, except at Loutra where the water is definitely unusually warm.

Pali This little fishing village is an excellent choice for those in search of fine beaches. Pali more than compensates for that which Mandraki lacks in this arena.
  The one road from Mandraki, to the mountaintop, passes by the turning down to Pali, which is reached by a steep, curving road and path down the hillside. This passes by the school and a tomato plantation, ending in the spacious village square, sprawling beside a fairly big caique harbour, protected from the sea by long breakwaters. Pali is peaceful and pretty, with a children's playground at the left end of the harbour, and a long, dark brown, volcanic sandy beach stretching away in the other direction (See Beaches).

The Volcano Nisiros' star attraction is the dormant volcano which is named Polybates. Mythologically he was a giant who, following the great war between the ancient Greek gods and the Titans, was swimming away in defeat, when the sea god Poseidon hurled a huge chunk of Kos at him. The massive missile pinned Polybates beneath the rock, where he sighs and fumes until this very day.
  The volcano's most recent outburst was in comparatively modern times -

1522 to be exact. Up until then, the island had a 1350m high mountain in the centre, most of which was blown away by the explosion. Text books disagree on whether the volcano is now 'extinct' or merely 'dormant'. Perhaps no-one knows but it certainly doesn't look extinct!

The vast crater, created by the 1522 eruption, is best visited at a different time from the tour buses. The approach road passes by Emborio, up on the right, and then divides. One route leads to Nikia, the other drops down into the fertile crater, which is some 5km across, filled with fields, trees, and small farm buildings, many with circular threshing floors on their roofs.

A steep, smelly path leads down to the fumaroles, where steam hisses out of the cracked earth - watch your step (and your children!), as the ground is hot and soft. The only danger warning is a single, red plastic chair standing near the largest holes in the centre - a very surrealistic scene! Not far from this crater is a little taverna, with more plastic chairs, and a WC, which only opens when the buses are due. There are manifestations that parts of the volcano are being used as thermal power plant.

Emborio This sad little settlement has suffered greatly from depopulation, and is now almost totally deserted. A steep, paved path, painted with whitewashed patterns of snakes and flowers, ascends from the main road into a village of disintegrating houses and overgrown streets. The occasional lived-in home, or music from the village cafe, evoke ghostly echoes of the past, rather than signs of present day life.

Only thirty people live here now, and their well kept houses stand strangely between the ruins of homes long abandoned. The main square is bordered by a perfectly maintained blue and white church. The main street, spanned by crumbling stone archways, continues to the crest of the hill, passing a sparkling blue and white chapel surrounded by ruins. From the top there is a good view into the volcano crater. A cave just below Emborio is reputed to house a natural sauna, heated by hot springs. There is a ruined (very ruined) Byzantine fort and traces of ancient walls. Emborioio's two children travel around the crater rim each weekday to attend school in the other mountaintop village of Nikia.

Nikia Eighty people inhabit Nikia, a superbly picturesque place of narrow, twisting streets and whitewashed houses, with a more cheerful atmosphere than Emborio. Even so, the population is dwindling - telltale signs such as crumbling houses are obvious, and the villagers inform visitors that over 3000 Nikians live in the USA! The bus pulls up in the car park area, at the bottom of the village, and beside this square stands the school, far too big, by far, for its six pupils. Accommodation is available in the hostel, also bordering the bus square, but there aren't any private rooms.

A taverna, conveniently at the entrance to the village, serves cool drinks. Beyond this, the steep, narrow street, painted similarly to Emborio's with snakes and flowers, twists up beyond the main square and a church. It terminates on a small square at the top of the village, from whence there is a fantastic vista, right into the volcano crater. It is possible to walk down a steep but well maintained path into the crater, with its central, bubbling hole. The walk down takes about twenty-five minutes down, and about twice as long coming back.

Avlaki Just before the Mandraki to Nikia road ends, an intriguing looking cement track takes off to the left, down the mountainside. On island maps the destination is marked as Avlaki, a tiny hamlet where fishermen from the mountain used to spend their summers. No one lives there now, although a couple of the houses are kept in reasonable repair. The 5km route soon becomes unpaved, after passing through the remains of an empty, ruined 'suburb' of Nikia. The views back towards Nikia, up on the hillside above, are spectacular. Watch for snakes... and cattle. At the bottom is Avlaki, which has a large white chapel, ruined buildings, a small natural harbour, and no beach, though it is possible to swim from the rocks.

Excursions
Yiali This offshore islet can be reached by a twenty minute boat trip from Mandraki. It has a golden sandy beach, in addition to a lot of pumice stone and mining machinery! The famous Greek admiral Miaoulis harboured here during the 1821 revolution, and, if you really wish, it is possible to see the well he dug 'when his freet (*sic*) was anchored in the bay', as the island tourist brochure puts it. Shops in Mandraki advertise trips to Yiali, or it is possible to simply hitch a lift with the daily boat which transports workers to the mine.

Island Customs, Feasts, Specialities and History
Religious Festivals These include the feast of Agios Nikitas, at the small church beside the harbour, on June 21st; Agios Apostolli, in Pali, on June 29th; the festival of Agios Panteleimonas, at Nikia, on July 27th; and large celebrations at the monastery in Mandraki for the feast of Panagia, on August 15th.
Most of the festivals are followed by food and dancing, in the centre of Mandraki, to which visitors are welcome. This is no tourist display, and no-one wears traditional dress - but the islanders, young and old, enjoy themselves no-end. ances typical to the island include the traditional step 'Embros' ('forward'), set to local tunes, as well as the 'Sirtos' or 'Kritikos'.

Wedding Customs Nisiros shares the Dodecanese custom of inheritance through the female line. The heir is the first daughter, the 'nikokira' ('land-lady'), and the legacy is granted to her not by her father, but by her mother. She remains the mistress and the manager of the family farmlands, which are in turn passed on to her own first daughter. Any land belonging to the father passes to the second daughter. Other children in the family are only entitled to wealth or lands which were gained during their parents' marriage, rather than inherited. These traditions are no longer rigidly adhered to, but they were still observed until the end of the 1950s. The purpose of these strict 'rules' was to prevent the division, and subsequent sub-division of large family holdings.
Arranged marriages were also traditional up to the 1950s. After the matchmaking, the parents of the groom visited the bride's home, where the proposal was officially accepted. Shortly afterwards, the groom provided

cloth for the bride's dress, and with the first snip of the seamstress, all the relatives threw down money for the bride. The betrothal took place in church, the wedding date, usually on a Sunday, was chosen, and the dowry agreed upon and read out to the relatives. The village musicians were sent off to proclaim the chosen day by singing to the community.

On the day before the wedding, bread, sweets, and firewood for the feast were prepared. In church, the bride's mother held the wine, and her mother-in-law the honey and almonds, which were given to the couple during the ceremony. A musical march home with candles was accompanied by rifle shots into the air, and singing and dancing continued until the Monday evening.

Handicrafts The particular style of Nisiros embroidery is displayed in the island museum, and can be purchased in the shops. The classic black, green and red patterns, embroidered by young women for their wedding trousseaux, have been carefully copied onto hand-painted pottery, which makes a tasteful and original souvenir to take home.

Local Produce Another island speciality is soumada, a thick, sweet, non-alcoholic cordial made from the juice of almonds. There are almond trees all over Nisiros, though many groves are no longer harvested and have run to seed since the depopulation of the mountain villages. When the nuts were an important product, soumada was a common beverage, but now it is only made by one old lady, Kyria Asimeni... yet another custom literally in danger of dying out. When she goes through a productive phase, it can be purchased at the liquor store and it is still served at the Delfini Taverna. The thick liquid should be diluted to taste. Interestingly, Lefkas island, in the Ionian, also produces soumada.

Other Traditions A few remaining island superstitions include the following: if a suitcase is left open in the house overnight, someone is going to die; you should avoid throwing out rubbish at night because you may also throw out your happiness, and when a child resembles his father, you should put an earring in his ear, or he will soon die. Those who looked into a mirror at night were supposed to turn into a vampire!

History Nisiros is one of those islands mentioned by Homer as having sent ships to Troy - an accolade which is cited in much the same way as an English village claims to have been mentioned in the Domesday Book!

Originally, it is believed that the island was joined to Kos island, which may be the basis for the volcano legend. At that time, a tribe called Nisiri lived on Kos, whilst in around 800 BC Nisiros was permanently settled by the Dorians. Later the island came under the rule of Rhodes, and the Knights of St John. The Turks established their suzerainty in 1533, and despite a few uprisings, lasted until the end of the 19th century. They were usurped by the Italians in 1923, who, in turn, were relieved of their 'command' by the Germans until the end of the Second World War. Eventually Nisiros, along with the rest of the Dodecanese, was reunited with Greece, in 1948.

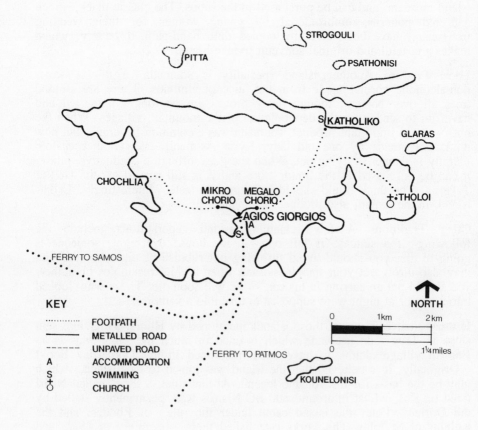

KEY

```
············  FOOTPATH
————————  METALLED ROAD
--------  UNPAVED ROAD
A          ACCOMMODATION
S          SWIMMING
✝          CHURCH
○
```

Illustration 10 Agathonisi island

On a scale of 1 to 5: Appeal: 3 Exploitation: 1 Beaches: 2 Scenic Beauty: 2 Accommodation - standard: 3 Accommodation - availability: 3 Facilities: 1	Sites to visit: 1 Accessibility: 1 Population: 130 Telephone prefix: 0247 Size: Approximately 5km wide, and only 2½km from north to south.

Location

The most northerly island in the Dodecanese group, Agathonisi is about 25km south of Pythagorio port on Samos, and 35km north-east of Patmos. It is only 20km west of the Turkish mainland.

Getting There

Airport: No.

Ferries: A scheduled ferry boat includes Agathonisi in its weekly, long haul expedition between Rhodes and Samos. The new quay allows this craft to dock alongside - in former times craft were met, in the bay, by a fishing caique, doubling as a passage boat.

At the time of researching the ferry was the FB Panormitis, a stalwart little ship, as much a supply boat as a passenger boat. It is absolutely reliable, and tramps the following route: Rhodes, Simi, Tilos, Nisiros, Kos, Kalimnos, Leros, Lipsi, Patmos, Arki, Agathonisi and Samos. It then backtracks thus Agathonisi can be reached from the focal islands of Samos and Patmos - but only once a week.

Supply boats also call in twice weekly, from Samos, and there is the occasional trip boat. In addition, there is an unexpected, weekly caique connection with Leros island, which is advertised in Leros' tourist offices. On the other hand, trip boats from nearby Patmos seem to be non-existent.

General

Despite being tiny and geographically remote, Agathonisi nevertheless possesses a vibrant atmosphere. The community is thriving, with a realistic opportunity of building a future on tourism, even though there is little sign of it at present. The island even has a paved road, two motor vehicles, a policeman and a doctor, not to mention electricity and running water! A village is slowly growing up around the church of Agios Giorgos, near the harbour, where the pensions, tavernas, and other modern buildings are situated. This settlement could well replace at least one of the old villages, in years to come. All the possibilities for future expansion are present as this is an embryonic, 'greenfield' site ripe for future expansion. It certainly will be sad for explorers when, and if, the first package tour company moves in, but it may well be the salvation of the island.

Agios Giorgos (the village is assuming the church's name) has a lovely beach of white shingle, and clear, clean water. It nestles in a deep valley between two high hills, the left one (sea behind one) of which is the hamlet of **Mikro Chorio** and on the right is **Megalo Chorio** village.

A paved road leads steeply up to Megalo Chorio, ('big village') where most of the islanders live. For defensive purposes, in days gone by, the place was almost completely concealed from the sea, sitting behind the hill. Megalo Chorio hides away two shops which sell everything and anything bought in by the ferries.

In fact, most supplies are shipped in, as is water when the storage tanks run dry. The wells are used to water the cattle and goats, but not to supply human needs. Apart from the farm animals, wild rabbits and pigeons supplement the demands for meat. Dietary requirements are augmented by fresh figs, as well as fish from the sea. The retired schoolmaster, who taught Agathonisi's children for forty years, is one of the island's characters. He advises that, the natives used to grow more of their own crops, and bake their own bread, but that doesn't happen any longer - "The women used to work. Now all they do is polish their nails."!

It is possible to spend an entertaining hour or so at the quayside cafe, watching the frenzied activity inspired by the weekly ferry boat's visit. Bread, mail, passengers, tomatoes and soldiers are unloaded, and islanders heading for Samos are plied with shopping orders for shoes, foodstuffs and the like.

Accommodation
There are two small pensions in Agios Giorgos, alongside the beach, each with five rooms, some of which boast en suite bathrooms. A few rooms can also be found in private houses, but all the accommodation is down at the port - there is none in either Mikro or Megalo Chorio.

Camping There is no official site, but the policeman does not trouble 'illegal' campers.

Food and Drink
Bordering Agios Giorgos quay are several tavernas where, in the main, the menu depends on the catch of the day, and how recently the last ferry called. The cafe nearest the quay is a good bet for breakfast.

Vital Information
Agathonisi doesn't have a post office or an OTE. Money should be changed before arriving and letters can be entrusted to someone to be put into the mail sack, before the weekly ferry boat departs for Samos. The telephone system seems to work better than on comparable islands, and the locals manage without an OTE   simply by using their neighbour's phones. (A common sound in the village of Megalo Chorio is the ringing of a telephone, followed by the shrieking of someone's name throughout the village.) If you require to make a telephone call, apply to the owner of your pension. In an emergency, the doctor has a phone, as does the police

station. The latter office is located in Agios Giorgos, on the right of the paved road to Megalo Chorio. The doctor's surgery is up in Megalo Chorio. Usually the doctor is a newly fledged graduate, serving his 'agrotico' year: all Greek doctors spend the final year of their training in a rural or island community.

Agathonisi's transport system comprises two three-wheeler trucks, used to carry people and goods up and down between the port and the villages. It is usually possible to catch a lift on one of them, especially after the ferry boat arrives.

Three soldiers are billeted on the island as a 'front line' of defence against Turkey, which is uncomfortably close.

Beaches
There is a very pleasant beach in the port - calm and quiet, with crystal clear water.

Sites to See
Mikro Chorio, situated on the hill to the left (sea behind one) of the port, has a few tumbledown houses, a few inhabitants, and no facilities.

Island maps are hard to come by, though there is one in the police station. The three walks worth exploring are to **Katholiko** and **Tholoi**, in the east, and **Chochlia** in the west.

Katholiko has a small beach, though you may have to share the location with a local farmer's cattle. Once a fishing hamlet, Katholiko no longer has any permanent residents, though fishermen occasionally moor overnight. To visit, select the track which leads up the hill out of Megalo Chorio and go through some gates. Keep left at the major fork in this track, as the right-hand path leads to the chapel of **Tholoi**, which is about a ninety minute hike from the village.

To reach the sea at Chochlia, take the path beyond Mikro Chorio.

Excursions
None, although the ferry boat's schedule allows for a day trip to Samos.

Island Customs, Feasts, Specialities and History
Religious Festivals These include the Festival of Agios Giorgos, in the port, on April 23rd.

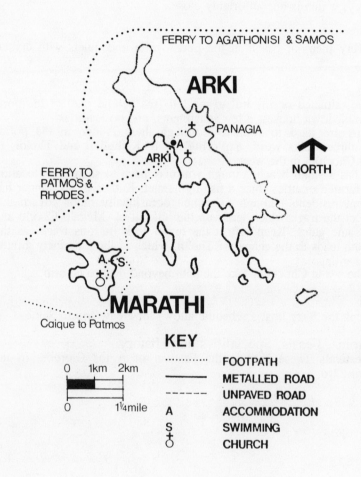

FERRY TO AGATHONISI & SAMOS

ARKI

✝ ⚲ PANAGIA

● A

ARKI

⚲ ✝

FERRY TO PATMOS & RHODES

↑
NORTH

A · S
✝
⚲

MARATHI

Caique to Patmos

KEY

0 1km 2km	
0	1¼mile

.... FOOTPATH

———— METALLED ROAD

- - - - - UNPAVED ROAD

A   ACCOMMODATION

S   SWIMMING

✝
⚲   CHURCH

Illustration 11 Arki & Marathi islands

On a scale of 1 to 5: Appeal: 2 Exploitation: 1 Beaches: None Scenic Beauty: 1 Accommodation - standard: 1 Accommodation - availability: 4 Facilities: 1	Sites to visit: 1 Accessibility: 1 Population: 40 Telephone prefix: Not applicable Size: Approximately 5km from north-west to south-east, and 1km in depth.

Location

Approximately 17km north-east of Patmos, 5km north of Lipsi, and 30km south of Samos islands.

Getting There

Airport: No!

Ferries: The only scheduled connection to Arki is a weekly visit by the scheduled ferry boat, which arrives at Arki approximately one hour after it leaves Patmos. (See Agathonisi island for the route description). This ferry's timetable allows a one day, or a one week sojourn!

Even this small ferry is too big for Arki, where construction work on a new quay has been continuing - or rather, not - for the last decade. At present, the boat waits in the bay, while fishing boats transfer goods and passengers ashore. Arki has no real produce, but fishermen can be observed passing up eggs and fish - Lord knows where these handfuls of goods end up - perhaps on the captain's breakfast table!

Other methods of reaching Arki require a certain knowledge and reliance on local help. For instance, every morning, in high season and weather permitting, a caique called Chrysoula makes the one hour journey from Patmos (known as 'the mainland' on Arki) to adjacent Marathi island despite the chalked-in destination board proclaiming "ARKI". From Marathi to the 'real' Arki is only a ten minute trip but a great deal of persuasion and dogged persistence is required to secure the passage, in a local fishing boat.

Anyone desperate to leave Arki before the ferry boat arrives could try the same tactic, in reverse, especially since the Arkian fishermen seem to spend many a morning relaxing at the taverna on Marathi.

Supply and fishing boats call regularly, and hitching a lift is a realistic possibility, but not to be relied on if a plane ticket is at stake.

General

Anyone contemplating spending a holiday on Arki must take the following into consideration: there is no electricity, no running water, no beach, no shop, no reliable telephone system, and there are very few islanders, let alone tourists. Manolis, a seventy-six year-old fisherman, still lives in the same two-roomed, stone cottage where he was born. "Here we have peace", he told me, "and flies", he added. But flies are not Arki's biggest problem, survival is. The island's future is shaky, to say the least. Only forty inhabitants struggle on, and although, in the past, they grew wheat and vines, there are simply not enough people left to make farming worthwhile. Arki has become barren, and depopulated.

A gently hilly island, covered with greenish scrub but few trees, Arki cradles its remaining population in the grey, low-lying, little village spread around the harbour. The families who earn their living by fishing, keep a few goats and hens to provide eggs, milk and cheese. Arki has two wells, beside the communal, stone, clothes-washing tubs and scrubbing boards in a seaside square. As the water is not pure enough for human consumption, it has to be shipped in, as does the bread.

There are three churches, one of them quite large, but there isn't a priest, nor a graveyard - "When we die, they ship us off to Patmos", says Manolis philosophically. He explains the lack of a priest even more pragmatically. "There are no priests because we have no young women here."! There is a police house, but no policeman, and no army presence, despite the island's proximity to Turkey. Education is provided by one small school with five pupils - when Manolis attended there were forty. At the age of twelve, children go to Patmos, if their parents can afford it, or start fishing...

Many islands harbour delusions of grandeur, and the inhabitants point out that Arki is actually a collective title for fourteen different islets in the immediate area, of which the largest is most commonly called Arki.

Accommodation
Arki helps prove the theory that however isolated, remote and undeveloped an island may be, someone, somewhere will rent a room.

The owner of the island's one taverna lets out 'ultra-basic', yet apparently purpose-built, grey stone bungalows. These lie just beyond the pretty village church, at the bottom of the path leading up to Panagia, on the hill. The bungalows are 'quite something', with taps, but no water, oil lamps, and mosquitos 'in plenty'. They each sleep up to six but one night for two people can cost more than a room in Patmos, as the unit cost stays the same for one or six. It is best not to fall out over the price with the owner, since, in the absence of shops, he is responsible for ordering and providing all supplies, including water.

Camping There is no campsite and no beach.

Food and Drink
Arki has one taverna, gaily decorated with an abundance of bright paint and coloured gourds, as well as a small cafe. The menu can be (logically) deduced from a knowledge of the latest catch, and the length of time between the meal and the most recent visit of the supply boat. With no refrigeration, these factors become all important.

Vital Information
This is easy. There is no post office or money exchange facilities, no road,

no vehicles, and the radio telephone rarely works! And, as aforementioned, there are no officials of any description. Mail leaves weekly on the scheduled ferry boat.

Sites to See

A cement path leads from the port to Panagia, which used to be a village, and surrounds the church on the hill above the port. Now it is simply a cluster of crumbling cottages, where two small families make up the last remaining inhabitants.

The harbour has no beach, but small, deserted coves can be reached on foot - the entire island only takes a couple of days to explore. After exhausting these activities, visitors can fish, or join the locals who wade in the shallows, spearing octopi and catching crabs...

Excursions

Marathi island is attainable, as previously detailed, although there is no scheduled service between these two rocks. Marathi does have a beach.

MARATHI

On a scale of 1 to 5:	Sites to visit: 1
Appeal: 3	Accessibility: 1
Exploitation: 1	
Beaches: 3	
Scenic Beauty: 2	Year-round Population: 1
Accommodation - standard: 4	Telephone prefix: 0247
Accommodation - availability: 3	Size: Approximately 1km wide
Facilities: 1	by 1km long

Location
14km north-east of Patmos and 4km west of Arki.

Getting there
Airport: !

Ferries:
See Arki. Surprisingly, Marathi is far easier to reach than its adjacent neighbour, as a very small caique, the Chrysoula, runs a daily service from Patmos, in high season.

Her roguish old captain is a bosom pal of Pandelis, the taverna owner, and boosts the establishment's midday takings by ferrying out a dozen or so tourists for lunch. The skipper has a wonderful life indeed, spending the six or so hours on the island feasting on fish and knocking back retsina. Anyone prone to seasickness should think twice about making the trip, in windy weather, as it is a little boat and the waves can be big, not to say mountainous. As the seas wash over the deck, the 'well-oiled' captain seems oblivious, chatting calmly with his mate, while passengers cling to the nearest support, and pray for their lives!

Note that the Chrysoula bears the 'lie' 'Arki', on the chalkboard which states the caique's destination but in fact it does not continue on to Arki.

The scheduled ferry boat, on its route between Rhodes and Samos, omits to stop at Marathi. However, when it drops anchor in the bay at Arki, Pandelis makes a rendevous with it, in his motor boat, which may, or may not be when guests are expected. Otherwise, take the caique which meets the ferry to Arki, and request a lift to Marathi.

When planning the homeward journey, remember that the 'daily' caique to Patmos may skip a day or two, and that it cannot make the trip during windy weather.

General
Part of the Arkian Archipelago, Marathi is the real answer for those seeking solitude, but are having second thoughts about Arki's basic disadvantages (but wait - that's what unspoiled islands are supposed to be about, isn't it?!). Never mind - admit defeat, leave behind the fly papers, candles, warm bottled water and non-flushing toilets. Comfort is at hand!

More a large lump of rock than an island, Marathi rises from the sea as a scrubby green hill, topped by a faded blue and white chapel. But it does shelter a long, curving, sandy beach - the likes of which Arki lacks. Fishing boats, from islands as far away as Kalimnos, lie at anchor in the protection of this quiet bay, which is indeed a haven of peace and tranquillity.

Pandelis, son of old Manolis from Arki, emigrated to Australia when a young man. He has returned to Marathi, with his family, and set up the taverna, a somewhat daring enterprise. This literally edges the beach, has rooms with running water and electricity, both installed by Manolis and his other sons. The Pandelis family, who are only 'at home' during the summer months, speak fluent Australian - a great bonus in such a remote spot. The island's only other inhabitant is a colourful character - an old goatherd who was raised here, and has no desire to leave. For some reason he is treated with great suspicion by the island's summertime residents, a feeling which appears to be reciprocated.

Accommodation
Rooms are available at Pandelis' taverna, and as he rather rules the roost, it is not a good idea to arrive with the intention of sleeping rough or camping. As the taverna is the only point of contact with the outside world, make friends with Pandelis or bust!

The price of his rooms, which have en suite showers and electricity, is 'average', rather than 'cheap', by small island standard. They cost about the same as a room of similarly good quality on Patmos. This may seem a high price at first, but it is worth considering the cost of providing the generated electricity and running water.

The *Twelve Islands* package holiday business has managed to locate this remote little spot, and it is possible to make reservations through them. Their presence means that independent travellers may not always have as much space as might be expected. In the 'shoulder' season there are usually empty rooms.

Food and Drink
Similarly, this is all provided by Pandelis, because, with no settlement, there is no other source of food or water.

His taverna serves mainly fish - excellently prepared, not cheap, but not overpriced either... and the salads are wonderful. It is tempting to spend more and more dreamy days here, feasting on good fish and good wine, a lay-over to be recalled through a haze of heat and retsina, blurred still further by noisy lunchtime debates between visiting fishermen, the caique's captain, and the residents. By contrast, a few steps away on the beach, the silence is broken only by the the gentle lapping of the sea... Those who require total relaxation and want to escape from all the distractions of civilization, should consider Marathi. It has to be admitted that it is not the cheapest small island destination, nor is there any island life to lend it a Greek village flavour. On the other hand there is nothing to spend your money on, except food and shelter, and as hideaway, it cannot be bettered.

Vital Information

There is no transport and nowhere to go. Marathi has no telephone either, but a VHF radio serves in cases of emergency. Ask at the taverna for any particular requirements.

Sites to See

Forty years ago, now-barren Marathi was home to several families, with their goats, wheatfields and vineyards. Today only the lone goatherd, who has a modern bungalow near the beach, lives here all the year round, with his flock.

Most of the island belongs to the all-powerful Patmos monastery. If you climb to the top of Marathi's hill, you can visit the tiny sailors' chapel of Agios Nikolaos, with its peeling, blue painted dome. Manolis has the key. Inside it is scrupulously maintained with simple dignity and hundreds of 'favours' dangle beneath the various icons. These 'thank you' gifts are from supplicants who were perhaps saved from a storm at sea, or survived an illness. Their gratitude is expressed to the saint who helped them, by hanging a symbol in brass, or a more precious metal, beneath his or her picture. The most touching items are those which were clearly individual treasures, such as wristwatches, rings, or other objects of personal value.

The tumbledown buildings surrounding the church resemble animal sheds, but were, in fact, the homes of the erstwhile island population. They are not romantic, which perhaps helps in understanding why everyone has deserted. To the back of the hovels, a concealed hole in the earth leads to a large, barn-shaped underground room. The captain of the Chrysoula claims this was a pirates' lair, dating back to pre-Christian times. Which bits of his tale are true I know not, but it is certainly very old, and would make a perfect hiding place for pirates of any era.

Excursions

None as such, but the frequent visits of the caique Chrysoula make an overnight jaunt to Patmos a possibility, if Marathi proves too isolated.

Patmos, the island where St John wrote the Apocalypse, is a picturesque place, with a brilliant white Chora topped off by a brown, foreboding, massive and still influential monastery. Equally influential to Patmos are the visiting cruise ships, gigantic liners which moor at the quay nearly every afternoon in the summer. These vast ships dominate the town when they dock, looming over the harbour and visible from almost everywhere. Their passengers make themselves equally obvious, and it is fun to sit in the harbourside cafes and watch them drinking their milk shakes, before the liner swallows them up and proceeds on its way.

After a few hours of life *a la* Patmos, you'll be glad to get back to Marathi....

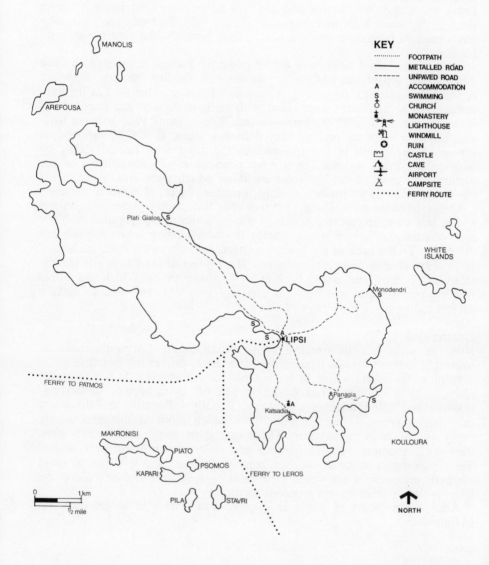

Illustration 12 Lipsi island

LIPSI

On a scale of 1 to 5: Appeal: 4 Exploitation: 2 Beaches: 4 Scenic Beauty: 3 Accommodation - standard: 3 Accommodation - availability: 3 Facilities: 3	Sites to visit: 1 Accessibility: 3 Alternative Names: Lipsos, Lipsoi Population: 650 Telephone prefix: 0247 Size: 7½km long, and less than 1km wide at the narrowest point

Location
Some 15km east of Patmos island, and 15km north of Lakki port on Leros.

Getting There
Airport: No, but Leros has one.

Ferries: In the summer months many trip boats cross every day from Patmos to Lipsi. The speedboat Anna is faster and less expensive than most of the competition, and tickets for this boat can be purchased at the general store in Patmos' main square. It is owned by a native Lipsiot and named after his girlfriend, from Nottingham, who sensibly spends her summers here! The ride between Patmos and Lipsi takes just over an hour. The regular, scheduled ferry boat includes Lipsi in its long haul, weekly route between Rhodes and Samos (see Agathonisi island for details). Sometimes another ferry calls. There is a caique connection with Leros, in high season, which may or may not survive.

General
Lipsi presents a sparkling face to visitors as they sail into port: a spick and span, blue and white town, dominated by churches. Everything seems bright and freshly painted: the blue domes, the caiques - even the fishermen's nets, spread about the quayside, are more vividly yellow than usual.
   The port is the island's only town, and a disproportionately large square, with marble statues, lies along one side of the quay, whilst the 'real' square, at the top of a narrow street, up the hill behind the church, is laid out with cafe tables and shaded by trees.
   One hour from Patmos by boat, Lipsi is often lumped together with Arki and Agathonisi as a rather out of the way, 'day-trip' destination. In fact, it is very different from both the other islands - much more fertile, and well farmed, with a reasonably permanent population who have even been granted a high school! Cows and sheep graze the fields, and the islanders grow tomatoes, as well as grapes from which they produce their own wine. A small fish-freezing plant, beside the port, does not mar the scene, in fact it adds to the encouragingly purposeful atmosphere. Lipsi is thriving in a way that other islands - many of them much larger - can only envy. Another

blessing the island enjoys is pure, and drinkable well water.

Tourism is quite clearly on the increase, and this attractive location, which has some excellent beaches, should be visited before too many others hear the siren calls. So far, the relatively low numbers of tourists are concentrated in the main town, and it is possible that it will take a long time for visitors to affect the scattered, sleepy, completely undeveloped agricultural hamlets. Lipsi is one of the islands where day trippers dominate, briefly, but whose true attractions emerge in the quiet hours after they have departed. It is a lovely place to stay.

Lipsi claims mythological links with Calypso, the enchantress who caused Odysseus a few problems on his way home to Ithaka. The main 'proof' of this connection lies in the resemblance with an alternative, olden-day name of the island.

Accommodation
The reasonably priced, well recommended Hotel Calypso is Lipsi's most pleasant and comfortable hotel, conveniently situated right next to the trip boat landing quay. Rooms have en suite showers.

Additionally there are a total of five pensions in town. A building behind the Hotel Calypso is simply labelled "Pansion", and the Pension Flisvos, around the bay, offers low price accommodation. Private rooms are signposted throughout the village, and there is usually plenty of space, except at the height of season.

Camping No official site, but there are lots of beaches. Most people choose to 'peg' their tents at Katsadia, as it has a simple taverna nearby.

Food and Drink
Lipsi offers a small selection of tavernas: the Calypso has a restaurant, and another nearby establishment is reasonably priced. The taverna behind the grand seaside square, and the fish taverna, beside the Pension Flisvos, only open in the evenings, during the height of the season months.

Outside of the port, Katsadia is the only beach with any facilities.

Vital Information
Considering its size and location, Lipsi does well for public services. There is no bank, but money can be changed at the Hotel Calypso, or at the post office, which is in the small, tree sheltered town square beside the church. The post office, which opens weekdays between 0800-1500hrs, also doubles as an OTE and there are two phone booths. The Town Hall, on the same square, houses the museum, and a somewhat elusive, tourist information office. If this is not open, ascend the steps alongside building, and ask for an island map in the municipal office.

The police station (tel 41222) is at the bottom of the flight of steps which leads up to the square from the quay. The doctor's clinic is situated on a narrow street behind the main church.

There is no island bus, yet, and transport is provided by a motley collection of jeeps and old trucks which meet the arrival of every trip boat.

Each vehicle bears the chalked up name of a beach to which they whisk passengers, for a reasonable fee. Before you leap straight from the boat into one of these bumpy chariots, remember that (so far) only Katsadia has the facility for food and drink.

Shopping is not easy - there is only one general store, behind the fish freezing plant - and that's about it!

Beaches

Lipsi Port The nearest, and busiest, beach to town, **Lendou** beach, is a five minute walk beyond the Hotel Calypso. Follow the quayside away from the village, then cut across the dirt path by a taverna, to the street which runs parallel to the quay. This drops immediately to the pleasant beach. A large building proclaims rooms and taverna - but enquiries in the past have been met with a friendly shake of the head, and a "not this year"!

Katsadia Jeep and boat taxis frequently run round to this lovely cove, but it is also a gentle and scenic twenty minute walk from the port.

The track leaves Lipsi, to the east, winding between some primitive dwellings in a small fertile valley. It then climbs over a cultivated hillside, and down the other side past a chapel to the narrow sand beach set in a picturesque bay, with an islet in the middle. This is a popular place for unofficial camping.

The small Taverna Gabieri, on a low rise, serves simple, tasty food and has rooms. The latter are extremely cheap, if rock-bottom basic - guests draw their own water from the well for washing and flushing the loo! The menu tends to remain the same, every day, which can become rather tiresome after a long stay! The old patron is quite cheerful, even if his wife spends all her time grumbling and making amusing remarks behind his back. Other beaches include **Monodendri**, Lipsi's unofficial nudist beach, about forty five minutes' walk from the port, and the island's best beach, **Plati Gialos**. This very long sweep of fine white sand is on the north coast, about one hour's walk from the port, or you can take the 'taxi'.

Sites to See

Most places worth visiting are listed under Beaches. The small museum, on the ground floor of the Town Hall, is often locked, but someone upstairs will provide the key, on request. The best exhibits are the examples of Greek costume from Lipsi and other surrounding islands. There are a large number of shards (bits of vases) from the ocean floor, and a most curious collection of jars of 'holy' sea-water, brought back by the island priest from religious locations, such as the Mount Athos peninsula in northern Greece!

Excursions

Patmos and Leros are the easiest islands to reach. The owners of caiques can be persuaded to venture to Arki, or even as far as Agathonisi, if a visitor's stay is long enough to become friendly with the fishermen.

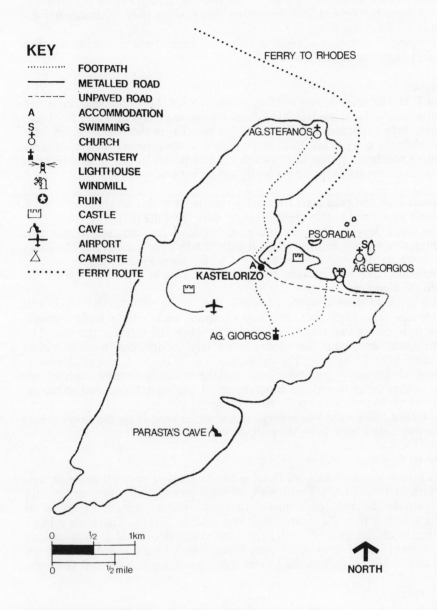

FOOTPATH
METALLED ROAD
UNPAVED ROAD
A   ACCOMMODATION
S   SWIMMING
      CHURCH
      MONASTERY
      LIGHTHOUSE
      WINDMILL
      RUIN
      CASTLE
      CAVE
      AIRPORT
      CAMPSITE
      FERRY ROUTE

FERRY TO RHODES

AG. STEFANOS

PSORADIA

S
AG. GEORGIOS

KASTELORIZO

AG. GIORGOS

PARASTA'S CAVE

0   ½   1km
0   ½ mile

NORTH

Illustration 13 Kastelorizo island

CHAPTER NINE   KASTELORIZO

On a Scale of 1 To 5:	Sites to visit: 4
Appeal: 4	Accessibility: 2
Exploitation: 2	
Beaches: None	Alternative name: Megisti
Scenic beauty: 3	Population: 200
Accommodation - standard: 3	Telephone prefix: 0241
Accommodation - availability: 3	Size: Approximately 5km long
Facilities: 2	by 3km wide.

Location
Although just 2km south of the Turkish mainland, Kastelorizo is 120km east of Rhodes, the closest Greek island. It is in the region of 500km from the Athens port of Piraeus.

Getting There
Airport: Despite the tremendous sea distances involved, Kastelorizo is easier to reach since the island was blessed with an airport. There are about three flights a week from Rhodes, in the summer months.

The construction of an airfield represented a last desperate attempt by the Government to boost the island's tourist economy, and to reassure Kastelorizons they were not forgotten. The airstrip is on top of Kastelorizo's mountain, where sheep and goats wander about the runway: presumably they are chased off prior to takeoff! The island's one motorised vehicle, the airport bus, transports passengers the ten minute drive to and from the port.

Ferries: Rhodes is the departure point for ferries to Kastelorizo. At present this craft is the FB Panormitis, the islanders' lifeline, making the six and a half hour journey twice weekly, summer and winter alike.

In theory, our 'old friend' the CF Kyklades also makes the Rhodes to Kastelorizo journey each week, a fact that encourages some visitors to bring along their cars. This is a pointless and risky exercise, because not only are there no roads, and nowhere to go, but the CF Kyklades, having called once, may well vanish into the deep blue yonder... rarely to reappear!

Greek aficionados will not be surprised to learn that, although Kastelorizo only benefits from three ferry visits per week, two of these are scheduled to arrive, not only on the same night but within a few hours of each other...

General A notice in Kastelorizo's small seafront square reads, "Well Come (*sic*) to Kastelorizo. Europe starts here." It feels like the end of the earth!

Kastelorizo is the most easterly of all the Greek islands - about twenty seven hours from Athens by ferry, but hardly a stone's throw from the southern mainland of Turkey. The island's one village, at the port, is strikingly picturesque, set in a deep, natural harbour, with tall white houses bordering the water's edge, all overlooked by the red castle on the hill, at the entrance to the bay.

This is one of the most intriguing Greek islands, maybe because its position has resulted in a traumatic and more than usually turbulent history.

A population of seventeen thousand, at the beginning of the 20th century, has dropped to the present-day two hundred, with most of the emigrants heading for Australia. There are supposed to be some seven thousand Kastelorizons in Sydney alone. The once wealthy city, which stood on the hillside near the castle, was destroyed during the Second World War, and much of the remaining town is falling into ruin. Many of the buildings are owned by ex-patriots, now living in Australia, who neither sell them, nor pay for their restoration. The locals bear an understandable grudge against these ex-islanders, who are unwilling to donate more, much needed funds to Kastelorizo. This goes against a national trend, as Greeks abroad tend to repatriate a great deal of money in their native islands. But then they are not usually next door to Turkey, and on the verge of total depopulation....

In short, Kastelorizo's outlook is bleak, and tourism would appear to be the only immediate means to survival, more so here than on any other Greek island, and that is some claim. Hence it is being officially encouraged, and with so few natives, even a few visitors are very obvious. Apart from the more conventional callers, others drop in by private or charter yacht, as Kastelorizo is a popular port of call on the way around the Turkish coastline. Tourists are arriving but, up to press, this 'way-out' little island can still be classed as unspoiled - just be sure to drop in soon, before it is either swamped, or totally deserted.

In the past, the inhabitants produced grapes and wine, oranges and figs, and, unusually, carobs in abundance. The latter still abound, so perhaps someone should tell the Kastelorizons how popular this sweet, dark brown pod is becoming, in American and European health foods, as a substitute for chocolate. You can break open the leathery cover and chew the sweet stuff inside, but beware of the fruit's laxative properties!

Accommodation

There is one modest, modern and comfortable hotel. Other accommodation is available in numerous, small, not-too-modern and not-too-comfortable pensions, though they are very cheap.

Those not offered accommodation on the ferry or the quayside, (and often there is so much frantic activity that even room owners become engulfed by the mob), should make their way around the deep, semi-circular bay. The nearest rooms to the ferry are situated in the back streets behind the 'promenade'. Immediately prior to the fruit and vegetable market (a large, open building with pillars in the front), is a narrow side-street on the left signposted to "Horafia" and "Mandraki", which passes between crumbling mansions. Where the road bends sharp right, after about 150m, looms the Rooms Kastraki. This is a tall, angular building on the left, with reasonably priced, rather dark rooms and shared bathrooms... if you can find the owner. Otherwise, continue down the same street to where it widens on to a dilapidated square. To the right is the Pension Barbara, a gaudily painted, three storey building, which from inside, and out, gives the impression that it is about to collapse. Once again the rooms are inexpensive, if basic, bathrooms are shared and the top floor has a pleasant wooden balcony decorated with flowers.

Other rooms are available in some of the tall houses back at the quayside and three-quarters of the way round the harbour, the crumbling Plateia Australias is edged by a general store, offering crummy rooms. At the rear of this square is a narrow side-street, beside the church, which leads to the big, solid, three storey Rooms O Paradisos. Alternatively ask at the Taverna International about the pleasant rooms in the 'blue and white' pension, at the far side of the bay, directly opposite the ferry boat quay. This accommodation has a shared bathroom, with constant hot water, and kitchen facilities which include a fridge. A disadvantage is that it lies across the water from an infernal disco, whose music booms across the bay... but usually ends by midnight.

The Hotel Megisti sits at the end of the left-hand promontory (facing seawards). En suite bathrooms and clean, pleasing surroundings make this a nice, if more expensive possibility. Because of the Australian connection, the hotel is often heavily booked in summer by Antipodeans returning to their roots, for a few weeks. Some rooms have balconies overlooking the sea, and the hotel's patio has steps into the sea for bathers.

Camping The island has no official campsite, and because there are no beaches, sleeping out can be a problem - it is certainly not viable in the main port! You could head over the hill into Mandraki, or hike to one of the rocky coves nearby, but in general, Kastelorizo is not ideal for campers.

Food and Drink

Tavernas are numerous, and of a surprisingly high quality, presumably because a large percentage of their clientele are yachtsmen (and women) who expect to pay for good food. The quality fortunate, as meals are not particularly cheap, by Greek standards, due to the added cost of importing the food. On the other hand seafood, which is usually highly priced everywhere in Greece, is abundant, and not overly expensive.

Most tavernas are concentrated around the Plateia Ethelonton Kastelorizon, the main seafront square. Many private craft moor against the quay wall of this Plateia, and the nearby tavernas increase their prices accordingly, that is with the exception of the excellent Taverna Lazarakis, in the front left-hand corner of the square (facing the sea). This taverna usually displays the biggest swordfish catch of the day, the carving knife is readily to hand, and their swordfish kebabs are both excellent and cheap.

The owner (whose intriguing wartime story is retold in the history section, at the end of this chapter) is in his sixties and, like most Kastelorizons of his generation, is illiterate. His two sons, in their late twenties to early thirties, are rare examples of island youth - they live here all year round. While the eldest bewails the lack of brides, the youngest is in despair about the future. He believes this is being stifled by Australians who hang on to their property, and put in further jeopardy by the fact that the two hundred residents have two hundred conflicting views about solving the problem!

Away from this square, the Taverna International, near Plateia Australias, has a good variety of food - even if Agapitos Benitis, the owner, can be rather moody. Try the squid stiffado, which is really excellent. Agapitos' lady friend, is very pleasant and she makes two of Kastelorizo's traditional sweets, stravo and katimari, baked with nuts and honey.

Several other tavernas are strung out along the quay, but for atmosphere, try the Taverna Platania, situated on the hill at **Horafia**, in the area just inland of the castle. By the by, all ruined main streets lead to this square, once the centre of the island's wealthiest district and still dominated by the enormous church of Agios Giorgos - reputedly closed for restoration (or is it simply closed?). This taverna must be the most desolate on the Greek islands. Approaching it by night, down one of the broad, disintegrating, overgrown streets, one senses the former grandeur of the area, now crumbling away and deserted. A few old people sit about, remembering better days. It is a sad and lonely place, but the food is good!

Vital Information

Kastelorizo has no bank, but money can be exchanged at the Taverna International, whose owner, the aforementioned Agapitos, is the island representative for the National Bank of Greece. Money can also be exchanged at the post office, behind the 'blue and white' pension and not far from the Hotel Megisti. This pleasant office, which opens between 0800-1500hrs, weekdays only, also doubles as an OTE. Unfortunately the island telephones are often out of order, for several months at a time. The same building as the post office, houses the police station (tel 29068), where a few soldiers, from the hilltop camp, are billeted.

Almost directly opposite, on the other side of the water, the doctor's clinic (tel 29067) is in the little square immediately prior to the ferry boat quay, whence a broad flight of whitewashed steps ascend to the ruined old town. The doctor has a 'tendency' to leave the island, and when this happens, helicopters are utilised to transport sick patients to Rhodes. Incidentally, Kastelorizo's fragile status is never more obvious than when a low-flying helicopter appears in the bay. Everyone, but everyone, glances anxiously towards the looming Turkish mainland, and wonders if the next invasion has begun. Above the doctor, is the Olympic Airways ticket office, where the staff of one speaks English.

Transport is non-existent, with the welcome exception of the airport bus, but then there is only one paved road - from the port to the airport. Unusually for Greece, there are few donkeys or mules either - most islanders travel by foot. Kastelorizo is superb for walkers, with footpaths ranging the length and breadth of this wild, barren little island. Shopping for food should be done as soon as the ferry docks, which is the only time the fruit and vegetable market operates - even though this may be the middle of the night! Some shopkeepers refuse to sell commodities (like yoghurt) to tourists, saving them for island folk, which is fair enough, if frustrating. A kiosk-type shop stocks basic non-food needs, and there are a few 'front-room' souvenir shops offering island maps, postcards, and other memorabilia. Look out for old photos of the town.

Kastelorizo's disco is housed in the cafe alongside the mosque, and due to the shape of the bay, the music reverberates around at night, which is a pity. Not that the disco appears to be very well supported, so perhaps one day it will close down altogether.

The port police are to be found in the large building sporting a prominent flagpole, also next to the mosque. They are the island's only source of information about ferry boats as there isn't a ferry boat ticket office. Tickets can be purchased on board.

Sites to See
The Mosque The distinctive red and while building, with its slender minaret, stands at the entrance to the bay. Built two hundred years ago by the Turks, it is just one reminder of the many invasions suffered by the island. The museum used to be housed in the mosque, but it is now only used for storage and usually locked.

The Castle and Museum
Kastelorizo's museum, exhibits everything from ancient Greek pottery to a one hundred year old iron, sponge diver's suit, and is far superior to the usual island museum - but then Kastelorizo's history is above average.

The collection has recently been rehoused in a restored part of the old fort - 'Castelo Rosso' (red castle) that probably gave the island its name. Originally the site of the Doric Nikogoras castle, the fort was rebuilt by the Knights of St John when they ruled the island from Rhodes, in about 1380, and used by them as a prison and place of exile for criminal knights.

To reach the museum, which is open every day (except Tuesday) between 0800-1430hrs, follow the signs from behind the quayside mosque. The curator shows visitors around and, on request, produces an old history book of Kastelorizo, written in both Greek and English and illustrated with excellent photographs. The exhibits are well displayed in a series of rooms around the central courtyard, where a chained falcon lends the location a certain air of nobility! Relics include decorated pottery from a 13th century shipwreck, a collection of regional costumes donated by a local family, and frescos from a chapel, which used to be part of the castle. Some of the most interesting items on display are old photographs of the island, and a drawing of the castle in its original state. Various rooms below have been restored as cells. Unfortunately the most valuable item unearthed, a gold crown believed to be of the Mycaenean era, and discovered in 1913, in a marble sarcophagus, was hastily shipped to the Athens National Museum.

By selecting the broad, walled, ruined street, which branches off to the right, immediately before the building, continues uphill from the museum. This eventually ascends to the top part of the red castle, which faces the brooding Turkish mainland, and boldly flies the Greek flag. Those of an adventurous nature can climb the metal ladder to the top of the high wall, from where a walkway leads part-way around the inside wall. Close to the fort stands a ruined mosque, a tumbledown windmill, and an ill-concealed, 'few-hundred-years-more-modern' army lookout post. The road along the crest of the hill eventually drops down between the bombed, ravaged streets into empty Horafia Square.

The Lycian Tomb If, instead of turning uphill, you follow the path beyond the museum and down the other side of the headland, past more   ruined cottages, it is possible to visit the Lycian tomb. This is the only such example extant in modern-day Greece, although several have been found in Turkey and throughout Asia Minor. To reach the grave, look for a steep, uneven stone staircase cut into the low cliff on the right, about five minutes walk beyond the museum. The tomb, which is at the top of the steps, is recognizable by the presence of Doric columns and a heavy stone entrance, through which lies the burial chamber.   Beyond the tomb, at sea-level, are excellent flat rocks from which to bathe.

Horafia The area known as Horafia, which literally means fields, lies around the wide, shattered square of the same name. The erstwhile centre of the wealthiest section of town, this square is bordered by the grand church of Agios Giorgos (built in 1902 to replace a church dating from 1632, with the same name) and by the atypical, Gothic style church of Agios Constantinos. The latter is currently the island's 'official' church and in the most frequent use. Constructed in 1835, the Ag Constantinos church roof is supported by twelve, granite stone columns from the Temple of Apollo at Patara, Lykia, in Asia Minor. Next door stands the oversized schoolhouse - far too big for its present role of thirty children - and, behind the row of children's swings, is the Town Hall, used for the occasional public functions.

Mandraki Leaving this sad scene behind, the road continues away from the main port by dropping down into Mandraki, a picturesque, quietly decaying community beside the sea. Most of the old mansions are falling down, though one or two have been restored.   Between Mandraki and the castle headland lies the modern desalination plant. Jutting into the sea beyond Mandraki is the island cemetery, where the great stone tombs are decorated in the typical Greek manner with photographs of the 'occupant'.
    The land side of the road is heavily wooded, and bulldozer tracks mark the site of a planned new hotel. Unfortunately the builder did not ask for planning permission, thus his efforts came to a halt when this was denied.
    If curiosity necessitates continuing to the road's end, you will be disappointed, as it leads to the island rubbish dump!

The Monastery of Agios Giorgos A rewarding walk, up the tempting if tiring zig-zag of whitewashed stairs, ascending the high cliff behind Kastelorizo town, leads to the originally named monastery of Agios Giorgos. Try not to make the same mistake as I did once - hiking all the way up, only to discover that the monastery, which is about a ten minute walk inland from the cliff top, was locked. The key can be obtained from the priest, who is usually to be observed early evening at one of the port's quayside tavernas, smoking and sipping an ouzo, decked out in his rakish, bright purple robes.

The view from the cliff-top over Turkey and the surrounding islets makes the climb well worthwhile. The path heads inland across scrubby moorland with a view towards an unexpected patch of cultivated land, where animals graze, close by yet another monastery. The latter looks interesting (through the keyhole...), but the walls are still impregnable to modern-day intruders not 'armed' with a ladder. This religious house is no longer inhabited, but is well maintained and houses the catacomb of Agios Charalambos.

If you have plenty of time (so getting lost is not a problem), why not return to the port by a different route. With your back to the sea, facing the monastery, a narrow path leads across the scrub, to the left, and winds over the heath. Follow this and, after ten minutes, select another narrow path, again to the left, which passes between ancient cisterns before descending across abandoned fields into a narrow valley where cows may well be grazing. You will observe the sea ahead, while the path dips to the left, descending steeply into Mandraki.

Paliokastro Another mountain walk leads to the site of the ancient acropolis on the top of Mount Viglo. Take the paved road out of town towards the airport. This skirts the lower side of an army camp, with lovely views over the red roofed town, then curves around the back, past 'innocent farmhouses', guarded by 'innocent' men, in army uniform. Pass the sentry and his box, on the right, and pick the broad, red and rocky stairs, which leave the road on the left to climb the mountainside. Steer clear of the vicious billy goat, which is sometimes present and attacked a friend of mine. Incidentally, she only escaped his 'attentions' by hanging her daypack on his horns, thus covering his eyes, and running down the mountain. A few days later the farmer retrieved her belongings, advising that the goat had hospitalised his previous owner!

This hazard avoided, the steps and path continue, via Cyclopian walls, to the ruins of an acropolis, dating from the 3rd century BC. There are numerous cisterns and a tower built of square blocks. Remains of a 3rd century BC Doric problem (temple gateway) are nearby. The site can be more easily observed - though at a distance - from the top of the airport road, which continues above a valley containing a few fields and the island's water reservoirs. From the top, there are great views over the nearby islet of Ro, and the Turkish mainland.

Agios Stefanos This is the next bay to the port - on the opposite side from Mandraki. A path behind the Hotel Megisti tracks the half-hour's walk, or a caique will take you. The bay is named after its little chapel (which is locked), and there is nothing particularly remarkable here... except that it is rumoured to be the future site of a de luxe hotel. A more unlikely spot could hardly have been chosen for what is projected to be a "traditional, two hundred bed hotel with dancing, taverna, disco, conference room, two swimming pools, a sauna, sporting facilities, and satellite television, working seven months a year, and costing £1,000,000 to build"! Not surprisingly, the locals are rather sceptical about the scheme, portrayed in the aforementioned glowing terms by a Greek business magazine, which also describes Agios Stefanos as having the island's only beach. Beach? Apparently the ambitious developers intend to build their own beach. They will have to construct an access road as well.

The islanders, who are somehow supposed to contribute, through regional funding, to the project, would in fact prefer the hotel to be constructed somewhere in the town, using present facilities, rather than as a self-contained unit over the mountain. Considering the vast numbers of mansions suitable for conversion, the whole dream seems very misguided.

Excursions

The Blue Cave (Parasta's Cave) Fishermen offer boat trips to many neighbouring islets, but if you only select one excursion, make sure it is to Kastelorizo's magical Blue Cave. This cavern has been favourably compared to the famous Blue Grotto in Capri but, not having been there myself, I cannot venture an opinion. Certainly the fisherman, who piloted me, claimed he had spoken to Italian tourists, who believed Kastelorizo's cave was better than Capri's!

The voyage takes about forty minutes from the port, and affords great views of the barren, rocky and inhospitable Kastelorizon coastline. The cave's entrance is practically invisible from the outside, and so low that to enter, even in the smallest of fishing boats, requires all passengers to lie flat on the bottom of the boat (lots of fun this, especially when the red hot engine has to be avoided). Inside, the cave opens out spectacularly into a vast cavern, with stalactites on the roof - and shining blue water, due to the refracted sunlight, giving the appearance of a giant's swimming pool, lit from beneath. There are no restrictions on having a dip, yet.... The sunlight results in bathers shining bright white, while fish appear black.

The cave's actual dimensions have been estimated as forty metres long, twenty-seven metres wide, and twenty-three metres high. Lucky visitors might find the resident pair of breeding seals 'at home', and in fact, one of the cave's names is 'Phokeale', or 'refuge of the seals'. Its more common, local name is Parasta's Cave, after a fisherman who reportedly discovered the location, whilst seeking refuge from a sudden storm. He must have been a singularly brave fisherman to attempt this entrance, in high seas!

Ro Of the fourteen named islets surrounding Kastelorizo, some only qualify as 'rocks', but each and every one is proudly declared Greek.

Though all are now deserted, neighbouring Ro gained nationwide fame due to its one female inhabitant, Kyria Despina, or the Lady of Ro. Despina moved to Ro, from Kastelorizo, as a young girl when she married a shepherd. The childless couple lived a solitary existence there for most of their lives. One night, her husband was kicked in the chest by a cow and he fell ill. Attempts were made to take him to hospital in Rhodes, but he died on the boat, between Ro and Kastelorizo.

For a short time, the widow lived in Kastelorizo, but then returned to Ro. Whilst in 'residence', every morning, Kyria Despina defiantly raised the Greek flag, in the shadow of 'Big Brother' Turkey, just across the channel. At sunset she lowered the standard. It became traditional for passing Greek ships to salute her with a blast of their siren. She eventually returned to Kastelorizo, for her last years, where she continued to raise and lower the national flag from her balcony.

There not a lot left to see on Ro nowadays - a few ruins of outbuildings, a chapel or two, and lots and lots of rock.

Agios Giorgos (the island) This is the islet with the beach. At least, that's how fishermen persuade the gullible to take the short trip by caique, to the little rock bearing one chapel and one house, just outside the entrance to the bay. The chapel is dedicated to St George (yet again), which gives the islet its name. In fact, although it's a nice little spot, the few grains of sand hardly constitute a beach. It is more like a gentle slope of rock into the water - good for bathing, but not a beach.

Trips to Turkey No, you can't get to Turkey... Amid great local outcry, the government banned 'shopping trips' to Turkey for cheap supplies. Old guide books assure readers that the 'illegal' trip to Turkey is possible, but it isn't now.

The official reason for the clampdown is that too many tourists, and their dollars, were unlawfully finding their way into Turkey. A more likely possibility is that goods of all kinds were being 'imported' into western Europe, via Kastelorizo, whose inhabitants have a nationwide reputation for smuggling. Whatever the justification, it is a most unpopular decision locally, since all foodstuffs, previously inexpensively available in Turkey, now have to be obtained, from Rhodes, via the scheduled ferries, at the higher Greek price, plus the extra cost of shipping. Taverna owners claim they have enough problems, without the government creating new ones, and go so far as to state they have no personal complaints against the Turkish folk, who obviously welcomed their frequent shopping expeditions. Incidentally, one suspects that certain fishermen still make the journey, since it was muttered that, if it was low-cost furs and skins we wanted, you know, they had a few in the back stockroom..!

Island Customs, Feasts, Specialities and History
Religious Festivals These include the feast of St George, on April 23rd/24th - a mega-event this, since the monastery, an islet, and two huge churches are dedicated to his honour. The feast day of the Agios Constantinos church, on Horafia Square, is celebrated on 21st May, and on July 20th, the islanders observe the festival of Profitias Illias, by feasting and jumping into the sea!

Wedding Customs In the days of arranged marriages, the father of the bride-to-be selected an appropriate husband; and then dispatched the matchmaker to the groom's house, to describe and praise the woman to the prospective in-laws. If they agreed to the proposal, the matchmaker returned to the bride's home with one gold coin.

The following day, the groom sent more coins and a bowl of sugared almonds, tokens which traditionally resulted in the dispatch of three diamond rings from the bride's family. (The less wealthy must obviously have adapted such traditions to fit their own pockets!). A few days later, the bride visited the groom as part of an official procession led by a man, bearing a pan of baclava on his head, accompanied by small girls with baskets of flowers. When the bride mounted the stairs, the children threw flowers, while sweets and drinks were offered to everyone. After these festivities, the company returned to the bride's home for a lamb feast.

Preparations for the wedding itself began on the Monday before the ceremony, when kouloures were baked. These traditional, round loaves of bread, with an egg in the centre, are still made every Easter throughout Greece. On the Wednesday, the bride's dowry was put on display, and the house filled with food, because from that day until Sunday, all the close relatives of the groom ate at the bride's house. On the Friday, children from both families collected herbs, which were presented to the bride on Saturday. Half of them were boiled for the bride's bath, and the other half were wrapped in cloth, and collected by wedding guests, who left money in their place for the children.

The Sunday church wedding, was followed by a procession to the groom's house, with singing and a grand fiesta. The day after the wedding, the mother of the bride and some relations brought boiled cinnamon and spices, milk and two stuffed chickens to the couple, and later, all the other relatives visited, bearing wedding presents.

Other Traditions Each year, on May 1st, every girl in the village cut flowers to decorate a bucket, then took it to the reservoirs to collect the 'unspeaking water of May'. The girls were not allowed to talk on their return to the village. Once they arrived, all the villagers had to wash in the water, and eat sweet cakes. This ritual was to ensure that May would go down sweetly, like the honey. Mistrust of the month of May is reflected in customs on other islands, and stems from the fact that the Turks conquered Constantinople during May, in 1453.

History The complicated, 'conqueror-follows-conqueror' history of the Greek islands is as but nothing in comparison to the turbulent history of this innocent looking little rock, so close to the territory of the old enemy. Kastelorizo has suffered dearly for its geographical location, in ancient history, and the 20th century alike. In the past one hundred years, the island has degenerated from a wealthy trading status to its present-day, sorry state, and anyone who sees the old photographs of the great town around the castle will surely want to know why? In ancient times, the island's first named settler was King Meges, from Echinada, the presumed originator of Kastelorizo's alternative name, Megisti. According to Homer, the island dispatched ships to Troy.

The first traces of man date back to 1400BC, and they are thought to have been Cretan sailors. The Lycian tomb gives evidence that the old inhabitants worshipped the Lycian Apollo, and the Dorians from Asia Minor were probably the island's first permanent residents - there are remnants today of the Doric language in local dialect.

In 350-300 BC, the inhabitants fought with Rhodes, in the Persian Wars, and remained under that island's rule until the ascendancy of Alexander the Great. Christianity was brought to Kastelorizo via St Paul and his teachings on the coast of Asia Minor.

In the 14th century the crusading Knights of St John took control of the Dodecanese, arriving on Kastelorizo, in 1306. They rebuilt the ancient fort, and ruled for over two hundred years. The King of Naples took over, in 1450, but by 1523 the island was made part of the Ottoman Empire, despite two brief periods of Venetian rule.

Kastelorizo was the first of the Dodecanese islands to revolt against the Turks, in the 1821 War of Independence. However, in 1833, the islanders' loyalty was ill-rewarded when Kastelorizo was given back to Turkey, in exchange for the much larger island of Evia!

From 1856, the French were nominally in charge, and surprisingly the Italians did not want Kastelorizo when they took control over the rest of the Dodecanese, in 1911. However, the citizens, numbering some seventeen thousand, flourished quite independently, entering into a period of great affluence, supported by trading on important east to west shipping routes. The deep natural harbour was filled to capacity with merchant ships - so many that some had to be wintered in Turkish harbours across the water! Island shipowners built an affluent town with large mansions all around the area of the castle, and three huge churches were constructed.

Then disaster struck. With the outset of World War I, the island was occupied, for the allies, by the French, and then, as one local historian put it, "happiness and laughings disappeared, and unworriedness is followed by worries and the uncertainty of tomorrow". The French used the harbour to berth their warships, placing nets across the entrance to prevent enemy ships from making a sneak raid. Kastelorizo was bombarded from the Turkish mainland, homes were destroyed, and the great exodus began.

After the Great War, Kastelorizo was handed to the Italians. In 1927 a disastrous earthquake caused more islanders to leave, and by the Second World War there were less than two thousand people left. But worse was to come. In 1943 British forces took control and evacuated all remaining islanders, save a few shepherds, to Egypt for the duration of the war. While they were away, the hilltop city, with its broad streets, grand houses, and wide staircases were bombed, burned and totally destroyed. Stories as to how this happened vary. Some say it was all the effect of enemy attacks, but many islanders still believe the occupying British force burnt the town to the ground. This was either to disguise the fact that homes had been looted, or because the allies hoped to give Kastelorizo to the east, in exchange for something more valuable, and the burning was an attempt to dissuade the population against resettlement. Whatever the truth may be, Kastelorizons, unlike most Greek islanders, do not feel much warmth for the wartime British presence.

After this second global conflict, ill-luck struck yet again. This time it was the homeward-bound refugees who suffered, as one of the two ships transporting them back to Kastelorizon caught fire in Port Said. As present-day islanders still relate, several people drowned or were burnt to death. Eventually, nine hundred and fifty people returned and their reaction, on sighting their town's destruction, can well be imagined. There was truly nothing worth staying for, and the last wave of emigrants left.

Since then peace, but not prosperity, has returned. Despite the islanders' friendly feelings towards the Turkish people, in the nearby coastal town of Kas, there is a nervousness about Turkey's physical proximity. Rumours are rife that, if the population drops much farther, the island will revert to Turkish rule.

One cheerful wartime story, to emanate from Kastelorizo, is the tale of Mr Lazarakis. He is the owner of the Lazarakis Taverna edging Plateia Ethelonton Kastelorizion, which fittingly enough means the square of the Kastelorizion Volunteers. At the beginning of the Second World War, Kastelorizo was occupied by Italian troops on behalf of the Axis forces. They were instructed to keep the population under close surveillance - even to the extent of following the fishermen out to sea. One night, Lazarakis and his friends departed to lay their nets, with the Italians in close accompaniment. The Greeks managed to persuade their guards to proceed with them to the neighbouring islet of Ro, where they set about getting them drunk, in the monastery. Assured that the islanders were only going out to inspect their nets, the Italians did not take the trouble to follow them, a second time. Once outside, the Greeks quickly locked the Italians into the building, and escaped by rowing across to Turkey. Although the Turks were neutral at that time, they wanted nothing to do with a boatload of Greek fishermen, and every time they came ashore, they were sent away. Eventually, in despair and after rowing 300km down the Turkish coast, the Greeks smashed up their boat, then pretended to be the victims of a shipwreck. Forced, at last, to do something, the Turks dispatched them to Egypt, where they joined the armies of the Allied forces. Lazarakis himself ended up fighting at the battle of El Alamien.

KASTELORIZO (Anon)

My Kastelorizo, your hills are high
and beautiful the girls who prune your trees.
Your eyes are like the sea, your browns a meadow
here ships take shelter from the winter storms.
I see a cave there shining like the sun,
and there's a bird above it singing sweetly.

I've been as far as Karpathos,
I've sailed as far as Kassos,
but Kastelorizo my love
could I forget you ever?

Tall these houses all of marble,
broad the courtyards paved in stone,
for relatives to come and go
(nor friends of yours be ever far)
for all the travellers who pass
to stop, and eat, and take their rest.

PART FOUR
The Ionian

Off the west coast of Greece, the Ionian islands share a number of characteristics: they are well populated, generally green and fertile, with spectacular, exposed western shorelines and protected east coasts. Although they are not the typical, Cycladic 'blue and white' style islands, having few domed churches or cubic houses, and may lack the characteristic glamour, they are no less attractive. In fact, some travellers prefer the red roofs and gentle green mountains of the Ionian to the rather stark architecture and painful brown peaks so representative of the Cyclades.

Corfu, of course, is the best known and the busiest of this group, being extremely beautiful, and extremely crowded - particularly by British tourists. Zakynthos too has becoming very popular, and even Ithaca and Cephalonia are not without their resort towns.

Of the five islands described in this section, Lefkas and Kithira are the largest. Lefkas, one of my favourites, was almost unheard of up to five years ago, but is now fast becoming popular, and should be visited before it is too late.

Kithira, although an Ionian island, is far removed from the rest of the group, lying off the southernmost tip of the Peloponnese, on the way to Crete. As such, it has remained quite cut off from the others of the group, and relatively free from mass tourism.

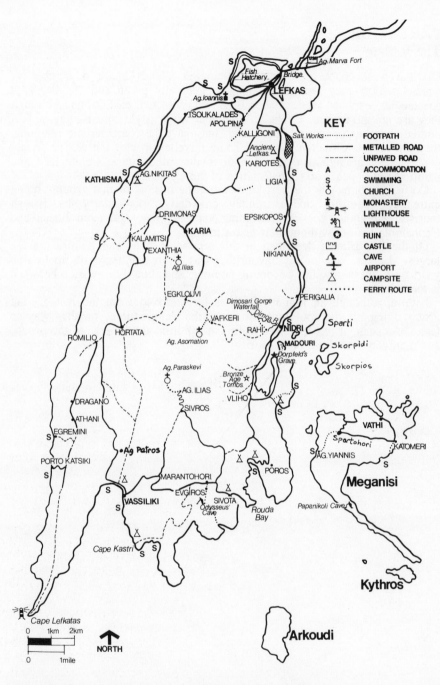

Illustration 14 Lefkas & Meganisi islands

CHAPTER TEN   LEFKAS

On a Scale of 1 To 5:	Sites to visit: 3
Appeal: 5	Accessibility: 4
Exploitation: 5	
Beaches: 5	Alternative names: Lefkada,
Scenic beauty: 3	Levkas, Santa Mavra
Accommodation - standard: 5	Population: 25,000
Accommodation - availability: 5	Telephone prefix: 0645
Facilities: 5	Size: 32km long and 13km wide

Location
Approximately 80km south of Corfu, Lefkas is now joined to the west coast of Greece by a bridge, not far from the mainland town of Preveza.

Getting There
Airport: No, but there is one handy at close-by, mainland Aktion.

Ferries: Lefkas is accessible by ferry from Cephalonia and Ithaca and boats link with these islands from the Greek port of Patras. Direct flights from Britain are now available to the small Aktion airport, also used by charter companies which are establishing themselves in the area. Olympic Airways operate a daily Athens /Aktion link.

Buses: There are four connections a day from Athens. The journey takes around seven hours, and the bus drives straight on to the island, stopping at the new bus station close to the harbour.

General
Although lovely, green Lefkas provided the original inspiration behind this book, a few years back, today it only just 'squeezes' in as an 'unspoiled island'. Of course, tour operators are still describing the place as totally undiscovered... but what are they doing there, if that is the case?

Nevertheless Lefkas, a large, well-populated land, absorbs its tourists well, with substantial areas remaining remote and unvisited. Furthermore, Lefkas cannot fail to please. 80km kilometres south of Corfu, it shares that island's natural attractions: from the rolling olive groves to high, western sea cliffs and spectacular beaches - a superb base for all kinds of visitors.

The island has three major visitor centres: Lefkas town, Nidri, and Vassiliki which I have chosen to treat separately.

Lefkas Town A lively and busy focal point, the town is not however the ideal place to stay, being removed from the island's best beaches, and more of a bustling commercial centre than a holiday resort. Its design is not stunningly attractive, with low houses and modern architecture, but earthquakes are common. The meccano-like structures of the church towers

may not   inspire rapture, but they are built to survive   the earth's next
attempt at 'reorganisation'. In fact, the historically frequent quakes are also
responsible for the lack of ancient remains anywhere on the island.

The town has one long main street, which leads away from the sea,
passing by a wide town square surrounded by cafes and old buildings. It is
at its most attractive during the glamour and excitement of the annual
Lefkas Festival (see Traditions).

Accommodation
A 'front line' of large hotels greet the new arrival, facing solidly towards
the causeway which leads on to the island. A couple of similarly modern
hotels edge the town's main street. All these are pleasant, impersonal, and
fall into this guide's expensive category. As aforementioned, Lefkas town is
not the best holiday base and although most of the island fairly 'bursts' with
rooms, few - if any - exist here.

Camping The island abounds with campsites - the nearest to Lefkas is 3km
away, at Kariotes beach, on the east coast, down the main Nidri road. A
further 2km along the same road is a more developed site, at Episkopos
Beach. Both are very close to the sea, and served by the frequent Lefkas to
Nidri buses.

To the west, the closest official campsite to Lefkas town is set in an olive
grove at Agios Nikitas.

Illegal camping takes place along the rather windy stretch of beach,
beside the windmills, on the western edge of the town's fish lagoon.

Food and Drink
An excellent selection of eating places vary from the posh, and not very
Greek restaurants, bordering the main street, to the smaller, absolutely
ethnic tavernas amid the maze of side-streets. Directing anyone around
Lefkas' narrow lanes is almost an impossibility, but try to find the
Lighthouse Taverna - it's good, and signposted off the main street, beyond
the town square. The owner speaks English and is extremely friendly. There
are several more ethnic tavernas in the same backstreet area.

Alternatively, the road beside the harbour is relatively newly completed,
and two or three pleasant restaurants and tavernas have already sprung up,
hereabouts, which will surely become the place to eat out.

At the entrance to the town's main street, a distressing number of fast
food stands have opened up. They seem to cater more for the town youth,
than for the tourists - but don't let the word 'fast' create any illusions!).

Vital Information
The main town square has a bank, which is often crowded. Best to head
further down the road (away from the sea), to a second bank, next to the
post office. This is usually less busy and also exchanges money.

All along the main street are small supermarkets, shops selling tourist
needs (postcards, snorkels, beachwear), butchers, general stores, *et al* and
at the very far end, various fruit and vegetable stalls. There are also a

couple of 'delicious' dairies, as well as a bread shop. The police station faces on to the High Street (what doesn't), and there are two or three travel agencies advertising a variety of trips and tours. A couple of waterfront travel offices offer charter yachts. The kiosk not far from the quayside has a metered telephone but getting a line is, more often than not, impossible as it is on almost every other island. The big OTE building is several blocks off to one side of the main street - take a right beyond the square and keep walking - the criss-cross streets eventually lead to the building, identifiable from the large aerial on the roof. Here, as elsewhere, the best time to make a telephone call is between 1600-1800hrs, when most Greeks are sleeping, although the office is open 24 hours a day. Close to the OTE is the island's hospital - down the wide street to the left of that building, facing the front door.

Bus connections to other island towns are very regular, and even the most remote villages mentioned have at least two buses a day. Links between Lefkas, Nidri and Vassiliki are very frequent (Kithira island take note!) All services leave from the new bus station, opposite the harbour. Taxis park both at the roundabout area, at the far end of the main street, and close to the bus station.

Beaches
The town beach is out beyond the bridge onto Lefkas, a strip of sand, well situated for watching the boats and yachts sailing into the canal. More beaches can be found west of the town at Agios Yiannis, and one rather wild beach, dotted by disused windmills, stretches all the way along the west side of the causeway which borders the periphery of the fishponds.

Sites to See
The Castle of Agia Mavra This fort stands just across the narrow channel, separating Lefkas from the mainland. Constructed by the Venetian Orsini, in 1300, it was later used as a strategic stronghold by whichever conqueror happened to be in charge at the time. In 1463 the chapel of Agia Mavra was built inside the castle. This was a 'thank you' gift to the saint, after the daughter of a Byzantine princess, travelling to Lefkas to marry the Governor, was saved from a terrible storm at sea. Part of the annual Lefkas Festival takes place here.

The Archaeological Museum
Unfortunately, visitors who are not conversant in Greek, or German, will understand little of the display, as the annotations and signs are only in those languages. This museum is dedicated to the German archaeologist, William Dorpfeld, who excavated an ancient site near Nidri (see History). Unfortunately, many of his finds were destroyed when the original on-site museum burned down. Entrance is free, and the museum, which is open in the mornings, is situated on Odhos Faneromeni, the road towards Frini. It is only just worth the walk out of town.

The Folk Museum
This is somewhat more interesting than the archaeological museum, and more centrally located, on a narrow street

between the OTE office and the town's main road. Entrance again is free, and the museum is open every morning, except on Sunday. Exhibits include examples of traditional Lefkas dress, besides a parade of full costume wedding dolls made by islander Eleni Katofori; a large scale model of a windmill; a loom; examples of traditional weaving and the famous local embroidery, as well as a host of household items.

Ancient Lefkas Some 3km south of modern-day Lefkas, on the road to Nidri, stand the unimpressive remains of ancient Lefkas.

Just beyond **Kalligoni** village, a short track on the right leaves the road, heading up through an olive grove to an ancient wall of large hewn blocks (numbered in modern red ink). Further exploration of the site usually proves unfruitful to the uninitiated. Although reference books proclaim remains of a theatre and ancient acropolis, it is hard to tell the difference between a modern day olive terrace and a bit of ancient theatre! The remains date back to 623 BC, when the town was known as Niricos and was occupied by the Corinthians. Excavations were made by Dutch archaeologists, but were never completed.

Excursions

Faneromeni Monastery Select the road out of Lefkas which winds up the hill, and eventually leads to Agios Nikitas. After some 3km is the small, pretty monastery of Faneromeni (or 'revelation'), worth visiting, if only for its excellent position with views over the town and causeway. The only monk now resident gives a guided tour to acceptably dressed visitors.

The monastery was built in the 4th century AD, on the site of an ancient temple to the goddess Artemis. The statue of the goddess is said to have shattered in two when St Paul visited Lefkas and ordained the island's first priest, Episcope. Fire has destroyed the building at least twice during its history. The present attractive condition is due to extensive renovations carried out between 1969 and 1974.

Karia The road beyond Faneromeni winds inland through the olive trees, until it reaches a junction prior to this mountain village. Karia is worth a brief visit - it is totally untouched by tourism, a fact which worries some of the inhabitants because the settlement is gradually depopulating.

Karia is the centre of Lefkas' unique needlework tradition - high quality embroidery, characterised by a geometric, closely stitched pattern and usually worked in gold thread on a cream coloured background. It is extremely expensive - a tablecloth costs around two thousand pounds, and has to be ordered about one year in advance. Small mats are more affordable. The number of embroideresses is dropping as every year goes by, and the young women have little interest in continuing the craft. Each piece takes many hours of patient labour, and this is quite literally a dying art, hence the high price. Pieces of embroidery (or Kentimata) can be purchased in Karia, or from a showroom on the main street of Lefkas town.

Mount Agios Ilias Just before Karia, a narrow road takes off to the right and climbs to the top of Mount Agios Ilias (Prophet Elijah). The summit is a weird mixture of beehives, a military communications base, vineyards, and a chalk quarry - the views are fantastic, but the foreground leaves a lot to be desired!

Agios Nikitas The picturesque village of Agios Nikitas was surely so much more pleasant and peaceful a few years ago, when the only access was up on down a steep track from the mountainous interior. The new road has resulted in ever-increasing numbers of tourists making their way here, and in peak season the beach becomes quite packed.

The village nestles in a small valley, protected from the rough west coast seas by a jutting headland. The broad, busy beach is of sand and shingle, with the shallow waters ideal for children. Agias Nikitas has rooms, a campsite, and plentiful tavernas, but lacks shops. If this beach is really crowded, one alternative is the long, rather wild stretch of sandy, Pefkoulia Beach, which edges the road as it approaches Agios Nikitas. Otherwise go beyond Agios Nikitas to:

Kathisma This is one of the best beaches on the island, and of the best beaches, Kathisma is certainly the easiest to reach.

The road between here and Agios Nikitas was paved in 1987, and predictably, these once deserted sands no longer answer to that description. As yet there is no development however, and Kathisma is so enormous that there is still plenty of room for everyone.

The road runs out behind a vast stretch of broad, yellow sand, with a couple of shanty type tavernas on the backshore, and the bluest of blue waves breaking on the beach. The sea can become rough even during apparently calm conditions, and children should be watched over, as the seabed drops away quite steeply.

Ligia 5km south of Lefkas, on the road towards Nidri, lies the picturesque fishing village of Ligia. Visit it quickly - it is a prime target for holiday development - but at present remains a beautiful little settlement. The quay is more often than not covered with dark red fishing nets, and a sight not to be missed is the dusk illuminated, string of fishing boats slipping out to sea, the smallest in tow behind the largest. So far, most of the cafes on the quay remain indigenous, but one feels this state of affairs will not last long.

The village has many many roadside rooms, a couple of small hotels, and a few discreet holiday flats. Eating facilities include one beach-side taverna, and there are some small shops and a petrol station cum supermarket. The narrow, white and pebbled beach stretches away on either side of the quay.

NIDRI Although Nidri has become the island's most popular resort, it still has an essentially 'small town' feel; for example, there are no large, modern hotels, and no sprawling suburban development either. Nidri attracts holiday-makers because of its ideal location, beside a bay full of tree covered islands. It is particularly popular with sailing holiday companies, who send windsurfers to Vassiliki and yachtsmen to Nidri.

If you dislike other tourists, avoid Nidri in the months of July and August. Otherwise, spend a couple of days enjoying the holiday atmosphere - bearing in mind that Nidri is the sort of place most guide books, and all the brochures, describe as quiet and unspoiled!

Accommodation

This is plentiful, although unfortunately for the island hopping traveller, much of it is reserved by tour operators.

Private rooms are available along the road in and out of Nidri, and nearby villages such as **Nikiana** and **Vliho** teem with rooms and small hotels. At a guess, there is more room-style accommodation on Lefkas than on any other Greek island, and the majority of these are in the Nidri area.

Camping The nearest campsite to Nidri is at **Desimi Bay**, about 4km away, on the peninsula, for which turn left just beyond Vliho. It has a taverna, shade, as well as shower and toilet facilities. The site edges a handy but poor quality beach.

The two campsites at **Poros** are better located. The more basic, less expensive of the pair is at the bottom of the bay, across the beach, and is the 'koinotita' or village camping. The larger Poros Bay Camping, which covers the lower part of the hillside, possesses much better facilities and also has bungalows for hire. (see Excursions)

Food and Drink

Nidri's most popular tavernas lie along the waterfront, with an unbeatable view, if not unbeatable value. Tavernas beside the main road, on the outskirts of the village, tend to be less geared towards the tourist population.

One favourite for excellent food, a pleasant location and good value is the taverna on the beach, a short walk along the sand from the northern end of Nidri's promenade. Unfortunately, but understandably the establishment fills up quickly, and as a result the service becomes very slow - but the waiters are friendly, apologetic, and run frantically between the tables in an effort to keep up with the crush!

Vital Information

Nidri has no bank, but the numerous tourist offices and the post office exchange currency. The post office is situated on the main street (at the Vliho end), as are most of the town's facilities. The tiny OTE office, as well as the tourist offices, which sell ferry tickets to Ithaca and Cephalonia, border this street. In addition, there are several general stores, a reasonably large supermarket, and a fair number of tourist shops, selling island maps and guide books (including my own guide book to Lefkas).

There are two pharmacies and a medical centre, a taxi rank, and numerous moped hire outfits, with a petrol station, just out of town, on the Vliho road. At the time of completing this book, Nidri has no police station, the nearest being down the road, at Vliho.

Beaches
Nidri's beach, typical of the east coast, is long and narrow, of white pebbles, and shaded by tamarisk trees. Windsurf hire and pedaloes are available, and a 'father and son' operation rent motorboats from the promenade. The nearest beach to Nidri, which is not just a narrow pebble strip, is at Poros Bay (see Excursions).

Sites to See
Bronze Age Tombs Such is the official name for these remains, which are signposted on the right side of the road from Nidri to Vassiliki.

Overgrown nowadays, the tombs and nearby foundations were excavated at the beginning of the 20th century by the German archaeologist William Dorpfeld. He spent much of his life trying to prove that Lefkas, and not neighbouring Ithaca island, was the true Ithaca of Homer and Odysseus. He believed this site to be the ruins of Odysseus' royal palace.

Surely onto a loser from the beginning, Dorpfeld nevertheless turned up some kind of royal remains, and worried the archaeological world for a while. On his side was the fact that Ithaca simply does not resemble the Ithaca described in the Odyssey (whereas Lefkas, to some extent, does), and no persuasive evidence of remains has ever been discovered on Ithaca. The name 'Niriton', which Homer quotes as an Ithacan city, also resembles 'Niricos', the ancient Lefkadian capital.

On the other hand, few poets are overly concerned about precise geographical detail - and there is the little question of the name....

The main street in Lefkas town is named after Dorpfeld, who is buried on the peninsula opposite Nidri.

Excursions
Skorpios The 'pack' of tourist agencies lining Nidri's high street offer boat trips to many places, and fishing boat owners run the short cruise to adjacent Skorpios islet and back, and it is well worth taking.

Skorpios belonged to Aristotle Onassis, and he and his ill-fated children are buried there. His son died a young man in a private 'plane crash, at Athens airport, and his daughter Christina was interred here in 1988. In her will, she left a legacy to the people of Nidri to allow a school to be built. Her funeral procession through the town was followed across the water by dozens of fishing boats bearing black sails.

Because Skorpios is private, no landing is allowed, although some boats stop to allow a brief swim in one of the coves of brilliant turquoise water. The excursion boats pass first by **Madouri** islet, former home of Lefkas-born poet Aristotle Valaoritis, whose statue stands in a small square near Lefkas harbour. He died in 1879, and his descendents still own the island. The most impressive feature of Skorpios has to be its harbour, for which many a Greek island would be most grateful - it is difficult to imagine this was all built for the use of just one man! Besides the large quays, there is a docking point that served Onassis' private car ferry (he actually had two) and a landing strip for his seaplane. Armed guards and large Alsatians dogs lounge around the water's edge. The monument marking the Onassis family tomb is to the right of this harbour, among the trees.

Further around the island, guest and beach houses are visible, as is a helicopter landing pad and the private tennis courts.

The Waterfall The waterfall of the Dimosari Gorge is an easy walk from Nidri. Take the road out of Nidri, marked 'Rahi and Vafkeri', and look for the sign which points the way to the waterfall, in Rahi. The walk takes about an hour and a half, along the dry river bed and past several small pools, which are suitable for bathing - at least in early summer when the water is still flowing.

Nikiana Heading north towards Lefkas town, the main road progresses, after ten minutes drive, to the seaside settlement. Until recently extremely sleepy and peaceful, Nikiana is expanding rapidly to meet the tourists demands. Nevertheless, it is still quite tranquil: surrounded by olive groves, in amongst which goats graze, and chickens scratch whilst the village dreams away between the green mountains and the calmest of protected shorelines. Countless houses offer rooms, in addition to the new and expensive Hotel Alexandros, besides a number of ideally positioned holiday flats spread along the narrow pebble beach.

Vliho and the peninsula 3km from Nidri is Vliho, located at the point where the peninsula takes off in a great curve from the mainland and, sickle-like, doubles back on itself. This village is remarkably attractive, with well designed houses, and a boatyard at one end of a long waterfront promenade. Here and there you may see a woman spinning, or walking along with a basket on her head.

There are rooms and a couple of tavernas, but the swimming is not good, and there isn't a beach. It is probably for this reason that Vliho remains quintessentially Greek and untouristy.

Turn left beyond Vliho on to the peninsula, where almost at once the vegetation changes, becoming thick and lush, with extensive fruit orchards. This road passes a right turn towards the campsite at **Desimi Bay**, then bends left and continues towards the peninsula headland, and the pretty chapel of Agia Kiriaki. Close to the latter lies Dorpfeld's grave - he died at Nidri, in 1940.

Poros Five kilometres beyond Vliho, a lane off the main road to Vassiliki sallies forth towards Poros and the fine beach at **Rouda Bay**. Follow the steeply descending road to the right, which winds sharply down the hillside. The beach is of large, smooth white pebbles, and is set in a deep inlet, with two campsites amongst the trees behind the backshore. The beach is not unduly crowded, except when a trip boat from Lefkas drops anchor.

VASSILIKI This is undergoing rapid development and the glorious little harbour village is in great danger of being totally swamped with tourists. Inter-island passenger ferries now dock, which adds to the already large number of visitors installed in the new hotels. One factor which attracts people, is Vassiliki's status as the best windsurfing location in all of Greece.

Its 3km beach, at the end of an inlet, makes for ideal conditions, in fact, one Australian magazine recently named it as "the third best site in the world at which to practise the sport!" Vassiliki makes a picturesque, well facilitated centre for a holiday, but you will not be alone.

Accommodation

Places to stay, in high season, can prove to be rather few and far between. The situation is not helped by the rash of new, stylish but pricey hotels, which have all been constructed within the past four years, as they are block booked by tour companies. Additionally, hordes of ferry passengers pour in to top up the average quota of visitors, but don't despair if you are unable to find rooms - there will be some available elsewhere on the island.

Camping The Vassiliki campsite is located 3km round the back of the beach, on the road to Agios Petros. It is a very pleasant spot, with a helpful, friendly, owner. There is bar and taverna, shower facilities, a few bungalows for hire and caravans are welcome. The site is ideally situated on the edge of the beach, and close by windsurfing equipment can be hired. Barbecues and other events are organized throughout the summer.

Food and Drink

Although the selection around the waterfront looks attractive, for some reason the standard of cuisine is rather poor compared to Nidri, and the waiters are generally unfriendly - unless you order one of their expensive fish dishes. The pizzeria on the corner of the quay is probably the best value for money.

An increasing number of bars are springing up between the more authentic kafenions on the harbourside, and there is even a nightclub...

Vital Information

Vassiliki still does not 'support' a bank, but there is a new post office, sited in the outer ring of the village, which exchanges money, as does the Hotel Lefkatas, on the main road. The post office also has some telephones.

The main street embraces numerous little tourist shops as well as a bakery, a couple of supermarkets and some tour offices. *Vassiliki Travel* sells ferry tickets and also offers car hire, though you may need to reserve a vehicle a few days in advance, in the peak season. Moped hire is available at numerous offices, as well as at the campsite.

Nearly everything a visitor could require is situated on the small stretch of road near the Hotel Lefkatas - except the police station which is located on a parallel street, one road further away from the water.

Beaches

The beach is vast and, as already stated, is a haven for windsurfers. This has some connection with thermal air currents, which ensure a modest breeze every morning, rising to a stronger wind later in the day, thus providing good conditions for every standard of surfer, from beginner to expert. It is possible to book a windsurfing holiday at Vassiliki, or to hire equipment on arrival.

The beach, while adequate, is not quite so ideal for sunbathers, as it can become breezy, there is little shade, and surf boards tend to dominate. But better beaches are only a short boat trip away (see Excursions).

Excursions

Agios Petros This mountainside village, above Vassiliki, remains untouched by tourism. Perhaps the newly added plastic toadstools, around the village square, are some kind of effort to attract visitors! Agios Petros is poor, authentic, peaceful and has marvellous views down the valley to the sea. There are a few rustic houses offering simple accommodation, a couple of tavernas, mainly serving souvlaki. Lots of old people and young children gather in the village square at night. Sometimes someone brings along a bouzouki to encourage the dancing.

This is a great place to stay for access to the best beaches, whilst retaining the peace and illusion of a deserted Greek island.

Porto Katsiki Until recently this location was only accessible along a rough dirt track down a cliff, but Porto Katsiki has now been added to the trip boat schedule, and is a spectacular sea journey from Vassiliki. Take the boat, hire a moped, rent a jeep - but get there somehow. This might be the best beach in Greece.

Backed by sheer, chalky cliffs, with a high bluff extending into the sea, Porto Katsiki combines the whites, golds, blues and greens of the setting to a dreamlike perfection which defies description. Some shade is provided by a low white cave. Take drinking water and any supplies. A few people camp in the wilderness. Those intent on escaping other visitors should hire a moped and visit in the late afternoon as the trip boats usually collect their tally of passengers, and depart by 1500hrs. This is the west coast of course, so the sunset is well worth the wait.

Egremni This is the site of yet another perfect beach, although with less character than Porto Katsiki. To Egremni's advantage it is wilder and more rugged - a long stretch of sand at the bottom of a tall white cliff. Nor, to date, is it visited by trip boats, so although it is a long, hard ride, the reward is fewer people and more peace!

To reach both Egremni and Porto Katsiki beaches by land, follow the road from Vassiliki to Agios Petros, as far as the left turn at **Komilio**. Take the latter, which eventually becomes unpaved, through the villages of **Dragano**, and **Athani** ('Immortal'). Just beyond Athani is a road to the right crudely marked "Egremni", and a little further on, there is a track to Porto Katsiki. Both approaches are rough and steep and moped riders should take extreme caution. There are steps down to Porto Katsiki beach, but reaching Egremni involves a difficult scramble, down an almost non-existent cliff path.

To the Lighthouse Selecting the above mentioned road through Athani village, without turning off to the beaches at Egremni or Porto Katsiki, leads to the lighthouse capping the spectacular southernmost tip of the island. From these sheer cliffs, in ancient times, the poetess Sappho leapt to her death nursing a broken heart due to an unrequited love. With this dramatic action, it is said, Sappho began something of a 'tradition'. A temple to Apollo was erected near this spot, and the priests had the habit of leaping from the cliffs in some sort of endurance test - or was it the forerunner of modern-day hang gliding? Admittedly, they strapped makeshift wings to their arms. Later on, local criminals were pushed over the same edge, and suitors crossed in love were advised to jump! If the criminals survived, they were set free, if the lover's survived they were guaranteed a 'shock cure' for evermore...

The white cliffs are stunningly impressive, and it is probably from them that the island took its name, as 'lefko' means white in ancient Greek.

Down below the lighthouse, international ferries plough their way from Patras towards the Italian mainland. This is a good place to watch the sunset, though the ride back in the dark is an 'interesting' experience...

Kalamitsi This hilly village, with its glorious beaches down below, is another of Lefkas' most secret spots, well away from the madding crowds. As in Agios Petros, shiny plastic mushrooms are spaced around a new cafe, in some misguided attempt to lure the tourists, but at present they have a lot of 'luring' to do.

The village is reached by following the mountain road north out of Agios Petros, and continuing straight on beyond the Komilio turning, almost as far as Exanthia. A sign points left to Kalamitsi, and a narrow, partly paved road descends to the village. There are a few rooms, most of them unadvertised, and a couple of tavernas, where the staple diet is souvlaki.

Women weave at looms, old men scrutinize visitors from the kafeneions - this is a glorious and peaceful place, with access to a string of excellent beaches. The main development is to the right of the junction, where the road enjoins the village; turn left and you can follow a narrow track down to the sea, where fabulous sandy coves are divided by large rocks.

Cape Kastri Leaving Vassiliki, in the direction of Nidri, the road passes a right turn, just before **Marantohori**, signed "Camping Kastri". Underneath, in Greek, someone has thoughtfully added "Take Care". They mean it - the rough track to the sea is 5km long, and it is not easy going. Eventually, after passing fertile fields and grazing cattle, the road reaches the sea and a secluded, white pebble beach. Some tents are pitched, but the only facility is a water well. Admittedly the setting is very pleasant, with a rocky headland curving around to the right to form a protected bay, sheltering a small sandy beach in the crook of its arm. The views towards Lefkatas Cape and the lighthouse are impressive. To reach the campsite 'proper', which is very unpredictable in respect of its opening arrangements, follow the track to the right, which leads to the site at the end of the headland.

Sivota This hamlet is signposted down a steep, paved but bumpy lane to the right of the Vassiliki to Nidri road. It has no beach, being at the end of a deep inlet, but is best known simply as a place to go and eat! In fact, it is so popular, that customers should arrive early if they want to get a table. The tavernas mainly serve fish and are spread out on either side of the bay. At night-time their lights reflect, fairy-like, on the surface of the water.

An unofficial campsite lacks facilities, and there are no rooms in the settlement, which lies along the right side of the bay. The protected inlet is popular with both private craft and flotilla yachts.

Island Customs, Feasts, Specialities and History

Wedding Customs Occasionally, a Lefkas bride still wears the customary bridal outfit - a colourful, long pleated skirt, and a bodice, angularly shaped by stiff board, which is pushed into the waistband to give a waspish figure.

Arranged marriages were the rule of the day until some forty years ago, and the groom and his family selected a prospective bride. If her family agreed to the match, they sent a suggested marriage settlement to the groom - a paper listing the bride's dowry, wrapped in a silk handkerchief. If this proved acceptable, the engagement was announced with two gunshots.

On the Tuesday before the wedding, the nuptial bread was prepared at the bride's home, and blessed by the village women, who on Thursday went to view her dowry. They brought with them almonds, wool to stuff the bridal pillow, and each sewed a red stitch into the garments on display.

On the Friday, the groom and his family visited the house with decorated horses, and took away the trousseau amid the congratulations of the villagers, who threw rice and almonds at the passing parade.

Presents were given out the day before the wedding, which until the 1950s took place at the bride's home, rather than in church. After the ceremony, a great procession proceeded from the bride's home to the groom's, where the mother-in-law greeted her new daughter with a spoonful of sweets.

The following morning, the groom fired a gun three times to announce his wife's attested virginity to the world, and the bedsheets were turned over, to the bride's mother-in-law for inspection ....

Special foods made for the wedding included melopita (honey cake) and sugared almonds.

Local Produce Almonds are used to make the traditional, non-alcoholic drink of soumada. This is a thick cordial which can be diluted with water, and is customarily drunk whilst nibbling dried biscuits. One taverna on the road towards Faneromeni from Lefkas town, serves soumada. The same drink is also to be found on Nisiros island, in the Dodecanese.

Costume and Handicrafts The old women still dress in traditional costume of a brown, wrap-around bodice and shawl, and brown, full-length skirt, with a kind of bustle at the back.

The needlework peculiar to the island is described in the section detailing Karia village, where the craft is centred. Other rural pursuits, such as weaving and spinning, are still crafted in most villages. One unusual custom is the women's method of carrying heavy loads on their heads, using a circular roll of cloth as a base for the jars and baskets.

Other traditions
The Lefkas Festival One modern-day practice is the island's Folk Festival -
an amazing display of dance and entertainment, which annually brings the
island to life during the last two weeks of August.   Probably the biggest
festival of its kind in Greece, the event, which dates back about forty years,
is featured regularly on national television.
  Much of the first week is taken up with cultural events - choral singing,
theatre and debates, mostly in Greek. Some performances take place in the
Castle of Agia Mavra. The second week is more colourful, being devoted to
traditional folk dance enacted by troupes from as far away as Sri Lanka and
Scotland; Hungary and the Ivory Coast. The dance festival begins with a
'barracola' - men's choirs singing on fishing caiques as they float around the
harbour. The following evening sees the grand parade through the streets of
Lefkas town. All the teams participate and the procession stops every five
minutes or so for all to dance a round or two, in the street! After two hours
the parade ends in the wide space on the promenade, close to the Hotel
Lefkas, where each team performs a brief routine for the crowds.
  After a break, during which the streets are filled with locals in national
dress, as well as costumed dancers from India, Africa and all over Europe,
the performance at the festival theatre begins. The venue is an open air stage
erected in a square, near the OTE office. This particular night, every team
puts on a display; throughout the following week, three dance groups
perform each evening in a show which lasts for between two to three hours.
When they are giving a show at the town's theatre, the groups tour around
the island villages. Most dancers are of a very high standard indeed, and the
islanders are justly proud of their festival. Tickets for each evening's
performance are on sale from two or three booths spaced out throughout the
town, both the week before and during the festival. Programmes are also
available, although the contents are not one hundred percent reliable, and it
is good advice to take along a cushion, as the wooden benches are hard.

History In ancient times, the island population worshipped the gods of
Apollo and Artemis, but centuries and earthquakes have combined to raze
all signs of their sanctuaries to the ground.
  In 625 BC, the Corinthians occupied the town of Niricos (Ancient Lefkas)
on the east coast. It is generally assumed, although not proven, that up until
that point the island was in fact a peninsula, and that the Corinthians cut the
first canal which separated Lefkas from the mainland. Under their rule, the
island was rich and a strong military force.
  Lefkas helped the Greeks during the Persian wars, and was an ally of
Sparta during the Civil War. In 197 BC, the Romans captured Lefkas,
following the battle off nearby Aktion, famed due to the involvement of
Anthony and Cleopatra. Incidentally, she fled and he turned to follow her,
thus losing the fight for the east. The Romans built a 700m long stone
bridge across to the mainland, with a central section of wood allowing the
passage of small boats - the larger Roman vessels were quite capable of
sailing around the western side.
  After the Romans departed, the island underwent the 'usual' influx of

nations - Venetians, European crusaders and, in the 15th century, a succession of Turks and Venetians. The Venetians must have won most of the battles, because they held onto Lefkas until 1797, after which Napoleon took over. Thereafter the island passed to the British, in 1809, who remained as 'protectors' until 1864, when Lefkas was reunited with the rest of Greece.

During the Second World War, Lefkas was occupied by the Italians, who were followed by German forces.

On a scale of 1 to 5:
Appeal: 3
Exploitation: 2
Beaches: 3
Scenic Beauty: 2
Accommodation - standard: 2
Accommodation - availability: 3
Facilities: 2

Sites to visit: 1
Accessibility: 2

Population: 2,000
Telephone prefix: 0645
Size: Approximately 5km wide
and 10km long.

Location
Around 6km south-east of Nidri port on Lefkas island, from where the ferries connect.

Getting There
Airport: No, but see Lefkas.

Ferries: The CF Meganisi links the island with Nidri (Lefkas) up to six times each day in summer - a surprisingly frequent service, but then the ferry has nowhere else to go. It calls at both of Meganisi's ports, **Vathi** and **Spartohori**. The former settlement is on the water's edge, whereas Spartohori village is a stiff ten minute climb up the steep hill, which looms over the port.

General
Meganisi is a quiet little neighbour to Lefkas, just fifteen minutes away by ferry, tranquil by comparison, and only known to tour operators as a day excursion from Lefkas. Few tourists stay, despite the fact that the island possesses excellent beaches, and its villages are quaint and picturesque.

Accommodation
Most of the island's rooms are unadvertised, although there are some more obvious places in Spartohori. In both Vathi and Kato Meri, ask around the cafes and the shops. Meganisi is hardly swamped with tourists, and space is usually available, even in high season.

Food and Drink
There are numerous tavernas, some of them well equipped to cope with the daily invasions of tourists, on round-the-island tours from Lefkas. If you choose to eat between noon and two, you may well find these strategically positioned beach tavernas crammed with customers - this is especially true of the taverna at Spartohori port.

Vital Information
The island's only bank is in Spartohori, which also boasts a post office, handling currency exchange. There is another post office in Vathi. The

police station is in Spartohori, where a couple of cafes have metered telephones, and most of the island's shops are located, including a supermarket, bakery, greengrocer and a couple of 'tourist supply' shops.

Meganisi has no public transport, nor moped hire, though that may change soon. However, distances are short, and hitching is a good way to get from Katomeri to Spartohori.

If you take your own transport, there is a petrol station in Spartohori, but traversing the narrow streets in anything larger than a Mini is a work of art! Generally, vehicles are not a good idea, as most of the island's roads are too narrow for comfort, and negotiating Spartohori's one-way system is extremely difficult, on all but a moped!

Beaches
Meganisi possesses good beaches - unfortunately those on the tapering south coast are only accessible by boat, but others can be found by following tracks eastwards out of Katomeri. These lead to a series of small coves, most of them deserted. Spend a quiet day here and you may well witness women washing their laundry in the sea and subsequently beating the clothes on the rocks to dry them. Other old ladies, dressed in brown garb, turn up to take what appears to be their weekly bath!

The beach at **Agios Ioannis**, on the west of the island, is 'just' accessible down a very rough track from Spartohori.

Sites to See
The **Papanikoli Cave**, on the island's south-west coast, is a large sea cave named after the Greek submarine concealed there during the Second World War. The submarine made surprise attacks on enemy vessels, even though Greece was occupied at the time. Since then, part of the roof has collapsed, but smaller boats can still sail inside, where there is a tiny beach. The easiest way to visit is on a day excursion from Lefkas town.

Island Customs, Feasts, Specialities and History
See Lefkas.

Illustration 15 Kithira island

On a scale of 1 to 5:
Appeal: 4
Exploitation: 4
Beaches: 4
Scenic Beauty: 5
Accommodation - standard: 3
Accommodation - availability: 1
Facilities: 2

Sites to visit: 5
Accessibility: 5

Alternative Names: Cerigo
Population: 4,000
Telephone prefix: 0733
Size: Approximately 25km long
and 16km wide

Location
South of the Peloponnese, not far from the mainland ports of Githion and
Neapolis, and on the ferry route between southern Greece and Crete.
    Although Kithira is a long way from most popular island-hopping routes,
there is no shortage of transport to the island.

Getting There
Airport: Yes. Olympic Airways operate several summer flights, each week,
from Athens. On the other hand it is best to bear in mind that these are
easily affected by even the most minor of adverse weather conditions.
Travellers should allow at least one day's stopover in Athens if wishing to
connect with an international flight home. Olympic Airways claim to lay on
cars to meet the planes (most islands provide a bus, but Kithirians appear to
be allergic to buses). Indeed, any form of transport from the airport would
be handy, as it is in the middle of nowhere. But, be warned, the availability
of these vehicles is questionable, and a taxi may be the only alternative.

Ferries: The ferry boats dock at two ports, Agia Pelagia in the north, and
Kapsali in the south. Craft arriving from Piraeus stop first at Ag Pelagia, as
do the car ferries from the Peloponnese. Ships continuing on to Antikithira
and Crete, or returning from those islands, may dock at Kapsali. If this
seems rather imprecise, the ferry boat ticket office is often sounds equally
vague, even on the day a boat is due. This is because the winds in the area
of the island are very unpredictable, and Agia Pelagia is a poor port at
which to dock in a breeze, let alone a storm.
    A scheduled ferry calls two to four times weekly, depending on the
season. It follows a somewhat complex route which takes in: Piraeus,
Kiparisi (mainland), Monemvasia (mainland), Neapolis (mainland), Agia
Pelagia (Kithira), Githion (mainland), Kapsali (Kithira), Antikithira and on
to Kastelli (Crete). During peak season months, the ferry also includes
nearby Elafonisi island in the schedule. This peculiar zig-zag pattern across
the Mediterranean is repeated, on the return journey. Because of the number
of calls (and a few unscheduled stops, which are sometimes thrown in as
well), passengers should make sure they know where they're heading - and
where the ferry is, at any given time! These arrangements allow voyagers

to pick up the boat at a number of mainland ports, between Piraeus and Kithira, as well as to choose their destination on Kithira. There is a twice daily car ferry from mainland Neapolis to Agia Pelagia, mornings and evenings. In the summer months, a twice weekly car ferry links mainland Neapolis to the small, north Kithira port of Platia Ammos.

Hydrofoils: As if the array of boating possibilities were not enough, Flying Dolphins (hydrofoils) visit Kithira four times a week in the summer, as the last stop on the Piraeus-Aegina-Poros-Hydra-Spetses run. They are twice as fast as the ferries, but cost twice as much. Note that the Flying Dolphins leave from the Zea section of Piraeus harbour, for which take the bus number 905 from the metro station.

General

Although historically considered part of the Ionian, Kithira is completely cut off from the distant, fellow members of its group, and now comes under the administration of Piraeus. Nevertheless, it shares the fertility of the other Ionian islands, as characterised by the green valleys, steep rocky gullies, clear streams, springs and waterfalls. As in Watteau's painting, 'Journey to Cythere', the atmosphere is one of verdancy and plenty - the very antithesis of a Cycladean island.

With many interesting places to visit and a few good beaches, Kithira is an attractive place to spend at least a week though, unfortunately, the island does have disadvantages for independent travellers. Primarily, there is an amazing scarcity of accommodation, not least in the ports of Kapsali and Agia Pelagia. Another difficulty is the dire lack of public transport - a significant problem on an island of this size.

Such an unusual paucity of accommodation and transport may be caused by the overwhelming numbers of Australian-Greeks who have returned to the island, from afar. They buy choice properties, and being generally wealthier than the native population, have no need to rent rooms, and little desire to encourage the tourist trade.

On the plus side, hundreds of people speak fluent English - in every taverna, shop or office, which does detract a little from the Greek flavour!

Because Kithira's two main ports function independently, I have chosen to treat them separately.

Kapsali

This strikingly attractive port consists of two semi-circular, back-to-back bays: the smaller one is picturesque, the other, the main bay is more functional. They are divided by a headland, on which are perched a lighthouse, as well as the 'inevitable' chapel. Above Kapsali looms the Chora and its giant Venetian castle, allowing picture views, in all directions.

Accommodation

The island's appalling lack of accommodation is at its worst in Kapsali. Frankly, you will be extremely lucky to find a room between early July and late August, and problems exist even towards the end of September! At least Kapsali has a campsite..

Three pensions, each with about two rooms, are situated around the sandy main bay. There are no advertised rooms bordering the second, smaller bay, so don't waste time searching, despite the situation appearing hopeful - all the pension-type houses simply aren't!

Another large pension can be located, a ten minute walk towards the Chora. From the bay, follow the narrow, steep street (not the back route) up the hill and turn first left off the road along a dirt track, ignoring the "No Entry" sign. The pension is at the end of this path, on the edge of a precipice, with a dramatically positioned, sandy beach at the base. If this is full, a tourist office down below, back on the promenade, offers more luxurious accommodation, in the expensive range.

There are a few rooms in the Chora, otherwise, resort to Mike, of Mike's Bikes - his business is signposted from the end of the ferry boat quay, and stands on a little square between Kapsalia's two bays. (It is also marked "OTE Office"). If there is any possibility of finding a room, Mike, who speaks fluent English, will be able to locate it for you. Good luck!

Camping Kapsali has one of the island's two campsites but both only open for the peak months. To get to the Kapsali site, of the two roads which lead up the hill towards the Chora from the port, select the back route. This passes into woods, and the campsite is pleasantly situated beside the road - beneath a cliff-face on to which are 'stuck' two white chapels.

The island's other campsite is far away, near the seaside village of Avlemonas (see Excursions, Kapsali for route). This latter facility is not a very good choice, being even more basic than the Kapsali site, and exposed to the elements of sun and wind, situated as it is across the road from an expansive but wild beach.

Food and Drink

Kapsali hardly bursts with tavernas either... The beach-side establishment, with blue and red tables, is nicely positioned, but the unhelpful owner tends to be surly, and it is often   infested with wasps. It is also festooned with signs such as "Don't touch the lamps", and "Don't sit on the wall"!. Unbelievably, the taverna doesn't even have a toilet. (Even if you don't believe it, there's not much one can do about it...).

The alternative eatery is in the sprawling building, at the end of the quay, where the owners are much more pleasant. Prices are reasonable, though the food is a little... well, a lot greasy. (But they do have a toilet!)

Actually, there is more accommodation, and better food, in Agia Pelagia, which is a pity, because Kapsali is a much prettier place.

Vital Information

Facilities are divided between the Chora and the port. Kapsali has a metered telephone, signposted "OTE" from the end of the quay and located at Mike's Bikes, one of several businesses offering moped hire. Shopping in Kapsali means the large supermarket near the end of the quay. When the owners close it down, to return to Athens, the taverna with blue and red tables supplies a few basic needs. The ferry boat ticket office is operated by a jovial old man who inhabits a little kiosk, on the end of the quay. He displays a suitably laid back attitude towards the probable, or improbable, arrival times of the ferries, and where they are likely to dock (at worst this is simply "we'll see").

Most administrative facilities are in the Chora. To get your bearings up there, the main road bypasses the town. Narrow roads from the bypass lead into the small, busy town square, characterised by a chapel with a bell-tower over the arched doorway. To one side of the square, a signpost points under an arch to the castle and the police station, which is a few paces beyond the archway. From the opposite side of the square, the Chora's main street takes off, up a gentle rise.

Just beyond the square, on the left of the main street, is the post office, which exchanges money (there is neither a post office, nor an official office for currency exchange in Kapsali). Ascending the hill leads past many shops, one of which is a large supermarket, which sells bread (the bakery is in Karvounades) as well as a wide variety of products, including tourist needs. A little farther on are fruit and vegetable shops, and a couple of pensions. The street passes beneath an arched mansion into a wide, large square, with a roundabout in the middle. Spaced around the plateia is a National Bank, which exchanges money, an OTE, a couple of moped rental outfits, a ferry ticket office and one office offering car rental. This square also boasts a real estate business... a lot of its offerings are advertised as "great restoration properties" i.e. crumbling Venetian mansions! The doctor's clinic is on the outskirts of town, beyond the museum. The Chora, as can be seen, is well endowed with facilities.

Unfortunately, public transport to and from the port is negligible. As it is a steep climb, or descent, best to give in and hire a moped! In the summer months only, a daily bus connects the Chora and Kapsali - it parks on the square, near the quay in Kapsali. As for getting from Kapsali, or the Chora, to the rest of the island, you can almost forget it. A bus leaves Agia Pelagia, once a day, for the Chora, and returns in the late afternoon, passing through most of the island's villages *en route*. During the school year, the only way of getting about is to use the school buses. These arrive in the Chora, in the morning, remain there all day, and depart for Potamos and Agia Pelagia, in the early afternoon. Wait at the bus stop on the main road between 1230-1330hrs (school hours vary, just to help) and quickly leap on, before the pupils tumble out of their classes. The journey is pure bedlam. One of the children collects the fares, proudly speaking English to foreigners. The Chora has the island's only high school, hence the daily performance.

Not surprisingly, taxis abound, and they are absolutely necessary.

Beaches

Kapsali has one long, curving, sandy beach, as well as a couple of deeper coves around the bay. The last and most impressive of the latter can be reached by climbing the steep hill road towards the Chora, taking the first dirt track to the left, which proceeds to the big pension, from where steep steps descend to an impressive gully between two rocky cliffs. On the main beach, pedalo boats and windsurfing equipment can be hired.

It is also possible to travel (by moped) to the two beaches of **Vroulaia** and **Fyri Ammos**, the latter being particularly worth visiting. To get there, select the paved road to the right, from half-way up the hill to Chora, as far as the village of Kalamos. From Kalamos square, signposts indicate the road to the beaches, which divides on the village outskirts, the left fork going towards Fyri Ammos, he right to Vroulaia.   I nearly always have great difficulty finding the way to Vroulaia, down through the olive groves to the sea, although there are signs, if you look for them. But in contrast to that of Fyri Ammos, this beach is not really worth the effort.

For Fyri Ammos, select the left fork, back in **Kalamos**, then simply stick to the main track, unless otherwise indicated. Where there is no sign, continue straight on (and try not to forget the way back!). There are dozens of other tracks criss-crossing this hilly terrain, as there are snakes! The last stretch is a steep, looping descent to the long, red shingle beach, beautifully situated at the foot of a tall cliff and with superb views across the blue, blue water towards Avlemonas, which is just visible over the bay. The beach is sparsely occupied but has no shade.

Sites to See

The Chora The hilltop settlement, known as the Chora or Kithira, has been the administrative capital of the island ever since 1537, when the pirate Barbarossa razed the northern city of Paliochora to the ground.

Originally, most of the town was contained inside the castle walls, with a lower settlement, Vourgo, on the north-eastern side of the hill, also surrounded by battlements. During the 18th century, the Chora spread beyond these, along what is now the town's main street, following· the contours of the land. A greco-modified Venetian architecture dominates the town - Venetian style adapted to the necessities of the location. The oldest houses are tall, their thick walls and narrow windows reminiscent of a fortress. Broadly speaking the types of homes can be separated into three distinct categories - the mansions of the nobility, town houses belonging to the bourgeoisie, and 'mews cottages' for the labouring people.

The tightly packed nature of the buildings and the lack of public space in the old part of the town reflect the defensive nature of the settlement.

The Kastro This structure was rebuilt, from older constructions, in its present form by the Venetians, in 1502.

Follow the signs from the Chora's small main square. These point under an archway, and past the police station, to a steep street which leads through the thick castle wall to the interior courtyard which is surrounded by ruined buildings. Those which remain in a reasonable state of preservation include the old Government House, four churches, a set of barracks, and the gunpowder magazines. There are any number of collapsing archways, and cannons. One side of the castle borders a frightening precipice and the views out over Kapsali are breathtaking. Even after the town spread beyond the fortifications, the population took refuge here in times of danger.

The Museum The Chora's small museum is worth a brief visit and entrance is free. It opens mornings only and is closed on Tuesdays.

The building is situated on the edge of the town, beside the main road, to the north. Exhibits include a few ancient relics, dating back as far as the Minoan period, and a collection of coins, which is particularly interesting - some bear the heads of Roman Emperors.

One of the oddest but most intriguing displays is a selection of 19th century English tombstones, dating from the island's period of British rule.

Excursions
(Also see Beaches)

Avlemonas In my opinion, Avlemonas is not as attractive as the nearby village of Diakofti, but it has character, and there is a vast beach, just ten minutes walk away.

Take the main road north from Chora, turning right towards Fratsia, beyond **Karvounades** (this is shown as unpaved on most maps, but in fact the road is surfaced to within 2km of the coast). **Fratsia** is half deserted and has a huge, empty village square.

Prior to Avlemonas, the road, bordered by fertile fields and olive groves, passes through **Kastri**. This is near the site of ancient Kithira, and the area has been excavated, the finds from which are displayed in the island museum. The archaeological remains are now totally overgrown.

The road continues across a dry river-bed, then detours inland, skirting a sea cliff, prior to rejoining the shore at one end of a very long, shingle beach, stretching a couple of kilometres, almost all the way to Avlemonas. Across the road is a campsite, in a wild, unprotected location.

Avlemonas is prim and tiny. Among the low, white, cubic buildings are two tavernas, one of which doubles as a general store, and the other closes by September. Ask at the general store/taverna about the village's few rooms, as most of them are not advertised.

Fishing boats are moored in two Lilliputian inlets, and a couple of tall palm trees add a touch of the exotic. The whole place has a toytown ambiance and even the octagonal Venetian fort, squatting on one of the promontories, is in miniature. This fort is slowly being restored and can be explored. There are a few cannons lying around, inside the walls.

The Western Corner and Myrtidia Monastery This large, luxuriant and well maintained monastery exudes an atmosphere of wealth and importance and is the most imposing church on the island. Strangely enough, although all tourist information raves about its significance, the name has been omitted from the current island map - presumably by accident!

The monastery is close to the hamlet of **Kalokerines,** in the south-west of the island. Take a left at either **Livadi** or **Kontolianika,** off the main island road. It is theoretically possible to do a circuit here, turning left at **Drimonas** and heading over the low mountains to the coast. This road, barely wider than a footpath, enjoys good sea views, and is cemented as far as the pretty and tree-sheltered **Agios Kosmas** monastery. From here the cement road continues... only to deceive, as following the surfaced route leads nowhere. (Presumably this stretch was sponsored by a farmer to gain access to his beehives). To reach Myrtidia, which misleadingly appears close by, it is necessary to turn off the cement road down a narrow dirt path, just after Myrtidia monastery hoves into sight. Walkers won't experience any problems, but those with a motorcycle will have to coax it over a frightening stretch of dust and rocks down a rather steep little gully. After which the track continues to Myrtidia. Incidentally, from Kalokerines the route is much more straightforward and paved all the way.

The monastery is indeed impressive. Peacocks strut around the lush courtyard and flowers bloom in every neat bed. Cells, available to pilgrims on the monastery's feast days, line the courtyard, so the place looks more like a luxury hotel than a religious sanctuary!

The most important yearly festival takes place on September 24th, the day when the holy icon was reportedly discovered. That this celebration is the largest and most popular, can be judged by the huge size of the car park, as well as by the toilets and water fountain outside the walls! The event occurs forty days after the festival of Panagia (the Virgin Mary), on August 15th, which is also observed. The golden icon of the virgin and child is blackened by age, and the detail of the face is obscure. However... during religious services, a chosen few 'see' through the obscuring grime, to vividly observe the face of the Virgin smiling joyfully.

The monastery was built in its present form in 1852, and thereby hangs the inevitable miracle. The architect discovered, after completing the first storey, that he was short of materials for the pillars, which were to support the second floor. He decided to go to Tinos for them, but storms prevented him from leaving Kithira for two weeks. In the meantime, his son experienced three dreams in which a woman instructed him to go north-east of the monastery for the stone. Eventually his father took notice of these visions and, lo and behold, they found the stone where she told them, and a miracle of Panagia was declared.

Limnaria This cove is signposted from the monastery car park area, down a firm dirt track. Although marked on the map as a village, there is only one house, and no permanent inhabitants, though five tiny caiques jostle together in a circular rocky inlet. There is no beach and no facilities.

AGIA PELAGIA

Getting There
See the beginning of the chapter. Incidentally, approaching ferries appear as though they intend to sail straight past Agia Pelagia, which can cause the heart to miss a beat or two, but it is only an illusion!

General
Kithira's northern port is busier than Kapsali. This strikes one as rather odd, because Kapsali has the appearance of a 'proper' port, whereas Agia Pelagia is simply a small, pleasant, but rather scruffy seaside village.

Importance has been thrust upon it because of the frequent ferry and hydrofoil landings.

The houses straggle along the waterfront, besides the tables of a few tavernas, and boatbuilding debris. There is much jetty-building activity in hand, as apparently the harbour is silting up. Construction is the 'order of the day', with the erection of many new houses underway, so much so that the whole village tends to wear the air of a busy building site.

Perhaps Agia Pelagia's most attractive feature are the views across the sea to the mountainous mainland, and the nearby island of Elafonisi, with a constant stream of great cargo ships passing in between.

Accommodation
Not quite so scant as in Kapsali, probably because Ag Pelagia has a larger, poorer, more indigenous population who are willing to make money from all and any visitors! Even so, rooms are hardly abundant and those that are available fill up during the months of July and August.

The tiny Hotel Kytheria, over a general tourist store at the end of the ferry quay, is more a rather expensive pension, run by a pleasant Australian Greek woman. The proprietor will help locate less costly rooms, if they are available - a big IF.

A few homes in the right-hand section of the village (sea behind one) offer accommodation, but there are no signs to indicate this. Continuing to the end of the bay leads up to the new, imposing, luxurious and super-expensive Hotel Apartments Marou. Turning left from the quay leads towards the Pension Pelagia, priced at the top end of the reasonable scale, but is less costly than either of the hotels. As there isn't a lot of choice, grab a room, any room, if it's free. These have their own bathrooms, added to which there is a beach shower outside, and it is ideally located, almost on the sand. A couple more private houses along this track offer rooms - and that's it folks!

The mushrooming construction does suggest that, in years to come, the availability of accommodation may be more plentiful.

Food and Drink
The best establishment is the Taverna Pharos, opposite the end of the ferry boat quay. This popular establishment serves an excellent variety of dishes, and delicious pizzas. The owner speaks English and his wife is Canadian, which makes a change from Australian!

The other restaurants line the seafront, in a long row, and the choice is far superior to that on offer in Kapsali.

Vital Information
The small supermarket, on the waterfront, sells stamps, as well as a reasonable selection of necessary items, and the shop next door sells fruit. The store beneath the Hotel Kytheria stocks the best island maps, as well as other tourist necessities.

Almost next door to the supermarket is a cafe with a metered telephone, and next door again, moped hire. The scooter man is, well, adorable... but the telephone number on his card is wrong, as I discovered once when I suffered a puncture, several hundred kilometres away. Fortunately he was most concerned for me but not the bike, which was abandoned elsewhere! The only other utility is the ferry boat ticket office, next door to the Taverma Pharos, which is run by a somewhat 'less adorable' character.

Other facilities are located a long walk away, in the larger town of Potamos, on top of the hill. Apart from a bank and post office, the town has both an Olympic Airways and, get this, a Qantas airline office. Did anyone mention Australians? Next door is a ferry ticket office. There are numerous shops around the main square: small supermarkets, a general store, which sells foreign newspapers; video stores (!); two butchers, and a bread shop, besides several tavernas and a few cafes. On Sunday mornings an extensive fruit and vegetable market is held in the square - so everything else, even the bank, opens as well. The only exception to this exceptional rule is the OTE office, also on the square, which opens daily, except Sundays, between 0730-1500hrs.

To the south of the main square, towards Agia Pelagia, is the island's sole pharmacy, as is a police station, which is on the other side of the street and best identified by the police jeep usually parked outside.

The hospital and a petrol station are on the outskirts of town, on the road towards Kapsali. Taxis park round the main square, and run frequently to Agia Pelagia to meet the ferries. As elsewhere on the island, public transport is a 'no-no'. Summer and winter alike, the bus leaves once a day for Kapsali. During the term-time it acts as the school bus, setting off from Agia Pelagia early in the morning (from outside the Pharos Taverna), calling at Potamos before heading south. This situation is bound to be rectified in the future, isn't it?

Beaches

Agia Pelagia's rather grey, messy, pebble and shingle beach stretches right around the cove. It is shaded by trees and thoughtfully equipped with beach showers. (They have beach showers - just no buses or rooms...) Because of the lack of accommodation, many people wild camp here in the summer.

Walking further around the bay, to the left of the quay, progresses to a couple of better beaches, also named **Fyri Ammos**, with red shingle and sand. These are broader, more private than the village beach, and the best place to camp, if needs be. For other accessible beaches, see Excursions.

Sites to See

The (Small) Cave of Agia Sofia This is not 'the' famous cave, but speculation says the two are linked... which seems rather incredible, as the other cave is on the opposite shore, 10km away. It has to be admitted the passages, which burrow deep into the hillside, have never been fully explored.

To reach this particular cave, look out for the sign by the side of the main road from Agia Pelagia, before the bottom of the gorge, on the left. It reads "Agia Sofia", and in smaller letters "Spili" ('cave'). A short path from the road descends to a miniature chapel which serves as a doorway for a staircase, eerily leading down into a very large chamber. For those who wish to explore, it is necessary to take a powerful torch. On the other hand, it is presumably dangerous to go too far into the passages.

Paliochora Barbarossa didn't leave much of this ancient, erstwhile island capital city standing, for visitors to see! He sacked and burned it in 1537, and Paliochora was never rebuilt. A few remains can be located beside the steep abyss into which, legend reports the Kithirian women threw their infants before leaping themselves, rather than be taken by the Turks. This was not a bad idea, since the few thousand islanders Barbarossa did round up, were sold into slavery.

Excursions

Potamos Potamos is reached via the scenic, paved route up the gorge from Agia Pelagia. The journey is worth the trip in itself - the road winds above the coast and the rocky gulf until it reaches the top of the mountain, flattening out, and passing lamentably, forest-fire-ravaged countryside, before plunging into a cool green forest. At the entrance to Potamos, on the right, is a large, old people's home built from local funds, of which the islanders are justly proud.

As detailed, Potamos is a bustling little town, especially during the Sunday morning fruit and vegetable market that edges the long main square. Many facilities are here (see Vital Information, Agia Pelagia), but there is no accommodation and, few concessions to tourists.

Platia Ammos There are two routes to Platia Ammos, which lies on the coast, about 4km north of Agia Pelagia. The shortest of these is via the dirt track from Agia Pelagia, that sets off from close by the Hotel Marou. This rough road passes between picturesque green hillsides, twisting and turning prior to eventually rejoining the newly paved road, which runs all the way to Platia Ammos from Potamos. The other route is described later.

The tiny hamlet has an oversized quay, where a car ferry from Neapolis docks, twice a week in the summer. The grey sand and shingle beach is large, and a few low cottages 'laze' beside the shore. There is one cafe, run by a friendly fisherman, and a taverna by the quay. Ask here about accommodation - there are five houses with unadvertised rooms in the village, which are usually full in peak season, but deserted out of the high season months. Platia Ammos has no shops, and the bus does not visit but taxis meet the ferry and can be 'hailed' by using the taverna telephone.

The alternative route back to Potamos passes through:

Karavas The road enters Karavas from Potamos under a triumphal archway. This village is quite delightful, its red roofed, whitewashed houses are set in a deep, green valley, overlooked by the large church of Agios Charalambos, built in 1876. The church festival is on February 10th, when Karavas is at its prettiest, being surrounded by early almond blossom.

The village supports a cafe, but no tourist facilities. If desperate for accommodation, make enquiries of the old lady in the house by the church as there are three rooms, behind the church, which belong to the village.

They are let out on the church's approval, and guests pay what they consider reasonable.

The view down the valley takes in two settlements on the opposite side which are now in ruins, is except for a couple of whitewashed houses that have been restored by foreigners.

The narrow street beyond the church, and along the valley, leads to the area's famous springs, the water of which is believed to possess healing properties. Not far from Karavas, on the west coast, is a track which leads to the sea at **Kalathaki**. Here is the spring Routsounas, famed for curing stomach ailments.

Milopotamos Many of the island's inland villages are pretty, endearing, enticing - but what do you do once you've walked around the main square and had a coffee at the cafe? Unless you're an artist, or an avid walker, you simply take a few photographs and then move on. Well, Milopotamos has a lot more to offer than most - at least one full day of exploration!

From Agia Pelagia, select the main Kapsali road towards the south, passing through fields, followed by areas of moorland. The turning right to **Areoi** and Milopotamos is clearly signposted.

Milopotamos is a truly lovely location, with a stream rushing through the deep little valley, and a shady square by the church where ducks peck around visitors feet. The cafe across the street from the square only serves food in high season. Outside of these months it doesn't even have bread for breakfast. There are no other tavernas or, for that matter, accommodation in the village. There are no shops either as the inhabitants patronise the mobile vegetable and fruit wagons.

Milopotamos means 'Mill River' - a reference to watermills of bygone days, which were used to grind flour. In the 1930s, there were still some twenty-four of them but none are now in operation, though one or two ruins can be seen.

After exploring the village, select the short walk to **Neriada** - literally 'Water Nymphs' - a waterfall "where nymphs live", as one old Greek guide book succinctly expressed the matter. The fall can be approached from both sides. The easiest route is to take the dirt track across the stream from the cafe. Cross the bridge by the church and turn left by the old mill house, around which are plum and apricot trees. The route passes by 'Fonissa', ('woman killer') - a name given to the spot where a young girl slipped and was killed, falling into the gorge.

After a bend in the road, a path to the right descends to a disused cafe straddling the bourn. Turn upstream here - you can hear the fall - and the narrow path leads to a deep pool beneath a fifteen metre high waterfall.

Even as late as September, this is still a worthwhile sight; it must be impressive indeed in the Spring, after the winter's rainfall. The pool is deep and wide enough for swimming, and one memorable feature is the thick, green moss below the fall. The abundance of water results in the valley being abundant with fruit trees and lush vegetation.

It is hard to imagine a spot more suitable for nymphs - beautiful, legendary female semi-mortals, who live to around one thousand years of age. They are supposed to appear at noon or midnight, and may invite a passer-by to dance with them. This is not a very wise move, especially if you are a lone male, as falling in love with a Nereid usually has disastrous consequences. They are fickle by nature, and young men who love them are prone to depression, strokes and seizures. In case this warning comes too late, the only way to make a reluctant nymph yield to a mortal man is to seize her by the neckerchief. At first she turns into frightening forms, but eventually returns to her own form and then succumbs. If you manage to keep the neckerchief, she may remain faithful for many years. Incidentally, it is also a bad idea to interrupt the nymphs at play, for those who do may become dumb, blind or epileptic. Probably the safest plan is to visit mid-morning or mid-afternoon, rather than midday!

Kastro Another worthwhile foray from Milopotamos is to visit the Venetian Castle, constructed in 1565, and situated, fittingly enough, in the district called Kastro.

To reach the castle, continue along Milopotamos' main street, past the square, keeping left where the road divides, and follow the signs to **Kato Chora** (lower village). The narrow street terminates on a square, decked with vines and bougainvillea. To one side stands the rather eerie, uninhabited Kastro.

A Venetian coat of arms marks the gateway into the maze of narrow streets, which evince unsettlingly recent signs of habitation. The paths are becoming overgrown, but gardens and trellises still exist. The locked chapels are still kept in good repair, the houses are tumbling down, but you can still enter them and come away with a persistent feeling of life in the Kastro, not so long ago.

At the opposite side of the castle, from the entrance, the walls overlook an impressive valley some distance from the sea. Indeed, the Kastro is rather strangely situated, being too far from the sea to provide any strategic defences, and distant from any harbour. Experts assume it was built by Venetian overlords simply to protect the farming families of the region, in times of invasion. The density of the houses, combined with the possibility of escape over the flat roofs, added to the fort's efficiency.

The houses are two storeys high, with no communication between the two floors. Exterior staircases to the upper storey, which housed the living quarters, form the arch over the door to the ground floor used for storage. Typical features include a fireplace in the corner, and stone window boxes of Venetian origin.

Unexpectedly, rooms are available for rent on the small square, just outside the Kastro, and impressive rooms at that. Knock on the door of the house which advertises weaving. This property is owned by a German lady who is in residence all the year round and weaves traditional island designs on a loom, a skill learnt from the old village women. Incidentally, one of the designs typical to Kithira is Cerotigo (Kithira's alternative island name is Cerigo), with a pattern of diamonds, probably derived from Cretan motifs. The weaver, Britta Frose, sells bags, rugs and wall hangings, which, despite being hand-made, are reasonably priced.

The accommodation, which is in the back of her house, are two comfortable, spacious, beautifully furnished rooms, with private showers and hung with weavings. Considering each room easily sleeps three people, they are extremely good value for money. A tempting and unusual hideaway from civilization.

The Cave of Agia Sofia In a sea cliff 2km beyond Milopotamos is the cave dedicated to Agia Sofia. There are better caves elsewhere in Europe, and this has nothing of the lasting glory of Kastelorizo's Blue Cave, but you will seldom find a more enthusiastic guide. A visit is recommended.

The cave or rather, caves, are only open on certain weekday evenings, and the times change each year. A notice in Milopotamos Square lists them.

Agia Sofia is well signposted from the village, the steep approach track being partly paved, partly unpaved, and partly a 'close your eyes and hope for the best' type of surface. It ends in a small 'car park', whence a footpath leads down the hillside, across a rocky stream bed and up a cliff face. The path is clearly visible and daubed all over with white paint - usually a reliable indicator that one is approaching a chapel.

The guide may well speak English. Each visitor or group of visitors is taken on a separate tour which lasts about thirty minutes. If nobody is around wait at the wooden door, outside which is a small, 'busy' generator. This enabled electric lighting to be installed in the tunnels for the first time, in 1988. The tour is a very 'Greek experience', and would probably not be allowed to take place in more safety conscious countries.

The caves extend to an attainable distance of 250m, and possibly much further than that. They were explored by the famous speleologists John and Anna Petrochilos, who also charted the Dirrou caves, on the nearby mainland. The caves have a constant temperature of 17°C, and are 'chock full' of stalagmites and stalactites, a sad number of which were broken off by unauthorised explorers, before the Milopotamos village authorities took the matter in hand. Inside the entrance is a small chapel and a rood screen, thought to date back to the 12th century AD. It depicts Agia Sophia and her three daughters, love, faith and charity, as well as a few more local saints.

Although publicity advertises "small lakes" inside, these are no more than tiny puddles. In the past the dripping water was considered holy and collected to use for bathing ailments, especially the eyes.

The caves are a series of chambers, some quite large, with the rocks shaded red, green and white, which mirrors the chemicals contained in the iron, bronze and calcium deposits. The passages between the chambers are the really exciting part, involving climbing, squeezing, bending and the occasional bumping, banging and boring. Some of the more spectacular rock formations have been named, the best of which is "the lion atop the elephant's back", in the final Chamber of the Lion.

The few light bulbs illuminating the gloom are augmented by the guide's gas lamp, and all in all one leaves with a feeling of accomplishment and bravery! The stories in respect of the true extent of these caves, which abound, are not taken too seriously, by most people, but have not been entirely ruled out either. There is a nominal entrance fee, which is well worth paying.

A large chamber on the hillside above Agia Pelagia (see Agia Pelagia - Sites to See) is also called Agia Sofia. Some say the two are linked by passages, but they would have to stretch the breadth of the island. Others believe that a connection with the cave of Agia Sofia, in the south, near Kapsali and off the road between Kapsali and Kalamos, is more likely, though it is equally distant. Certainly, these caves head off in that direction, and apparently some unfortunate cat, which accidentally entered one end, came out of the other. My duties do not extend this far but it is a challenge, for someone!

Diakofti To reach the seaside hamlet of Diakofti, take the main south road from Potamos, turning off left at the half-deserted village of **Aroniadika**, towards the airport. The road is paved through the similarly forsaken settlement of **Frilingianika**, as far as the airport itself. Since the airport was extended, the road has been re-routed to make an unpaved, semi-circular detour, which is not detailed on the island map. Beyond this the road is paved, prior to the asphalt surface 'expiring' altogether. The last 6km or so are unpaved, apart from a short cement stretch here and there.

The final approach passes by the large Agia Moni monastery high on the mountain. This is inhabited by a solitary monk but he is deaf, so visitors should bang hard on the door, and dress properly, as usual. The steep road up the mountainside is surfaced, and views from the summit are panoramic, to say the least.

The seaside village of Avlemonas, to the south, becomes visible away to the right of the Diakofti road. A rough, cross-country track joins the two roads (for a description of Avlemonas see Excursions, Kapsali). The soil of the plain hereabouts is a rich red colour, and indeed the area spanning the land between the two roads, is named 'Kokkinochorafap' or red fields.

The track cuts a great swathe, down the hillside, towards Diakofti, and the now visible offshore islet of **Makronisi**. The latter was recently joined to the land by a man-made causeway. The reason for the continuing construction work is that a second ferry boat quay is planned, but the sea is only deep enough for docking off the island, not the coast itself. When the weather is too rough for boats to berth at Agia Pelagia, they will proceed to this more sheltered spot.

Diakofti is worth the long journey. It is a fertile little settlement with a paradise-style, long, silver sand beach, backed by trees and a few white-walled, red tiled fishermen's cottages, bordering a glorious turquoise sea. Half-way along, a fishing jetty protrudes into the water, to which boats are moored. Even this tranquil hamlet, with only twenty 'year-round' inhabitants, has its share of Australian speakers.

There are twenty-five rooms, all of which are fully booked in the summer months. The friendliest and most accommodating family must surely be those at the Taverna Tou Manoli, along the seafront to the left of the end of the road. In the low season Manoli is as likely to ask lone travellers to share the family dinner, as he is to charge for a meal! He can offer a couple of rooms, and his family speak some Australian.

At the other end of the beach, the Hotel Kithira is more correctly flats, obviously built by a homecoming Australian expatriate as the entrance bears a great clock, in the shape of an Australian map! Probably the best place to ask for rooms is at any of the few tavernas scattered around.

Island Customs, Feasts, Specialities and History
Religious Festivals Feast days on Kithira include: July 23rd, at Agia Pelagia church in the port; 24th September, the major festival at Myrtidia monastery; 29th August, Agios Yiannis on the rock, above Kapsali; 6th August, Agia Moni; September 8th at Agios Sozondas church in Milopotamos;   14th September, at the church of Estavromens, in Chora; and February 10th, a fiesta amid the almond blossoms at Karavas' church, Agios Charalambos.

Wedding Customs Unusually, in the past the custom of the giving of wedding dowries extended to the groom, as well as the bride. The father of the groom had to provide a home for the couple, either by building one, or by signing away his own house, or at least a portion of the dwelling.

The bride's dowry was money, and her mother's family heirlooms. Her inheritance could never be seized or sold, even if the couple were in debt. The only sale of her dowry possible was to buy land, which would be in her name, and not under the husband's jurisdiction.

On the Thursday before the wedding, the bride's dowry was collected from her home amid great rejoicing, and transferred to their new house by a village procession of young people.

The actual wedding was never to coincide with Santa Mavra's day, nor should it take place on a Tuesday. A Tuesday still portends bad luck in Greece because the Turks captured Constantinople on that day, and Tuesday the 13th is the most unlucky day in the Greek calendar.) May was also discouraged as a wedding month - "only donkeys get married in May" went the saying. The most propitious time for a marriage was agreed to be just after any full moon.

Assuming the bride and groom finally sorted out a wedding date, both walked through the village to the church in an individual procession. By tradition the paths of the two columns had to cross somewhere. Following the wedding, a grand fiesta was held, with dancing and feasting. After which the couple went to the groom's house, where they would spend at least eight days (and nights) together.

Kithira's version of one of the less attractive wedding customs - the 'certification' of the bride's virginity - was for the groom's mother to check her new daughter-in-law's nightdress for the relevant 'signs'. On finding these it was to be fervently hoped, she threw golden coins onto the clothing, and her son fired a gun out of the window.

Occasionally, when the bride had no brothers, her husband was installed in her father's house as the 'new son', and began to manage the business of the farms and the land.

To have as many children as possible was often the goal of a marriage, especially as some offspring were not expected to survive into adulthood. When a woman had given birth, she and the child were considered to be supernaturally at risk for the forty day period between the delivery and the custom of 'churching'. To cheat the jealous demons, mother and baby had to sleep with bread under their pillows and a lighted candle burning night and day. Palm leaves beneath the pillow were also supposed to fend off any black magic, as were beaded necklaces about the baby's neck.

History Kithira is the mythical birthplace of Aphrodite, who sprung from the ocean after Zeus castrated his father, Kronos, and tossed the 'bits' into the sea.

The most sacred ancient temple to Aphrodite, in all of Greece, was on the island, and a few ancient remains of the sanctuary have been found in the area of Kastro, near Avlemonas. Because of its 'crossroads' position, Kithira was always important to old civilizations, but the Phoenicians journeyed here for something else - the murex or porphyrite shellfish, from which they produced a purple dye for royal garments. The Minoan civilization of Crete established a trading post, around 1600 BC, but the central situation had its disadvantages as well - pirates and enemy civilizations were forever on the attack, and Kithira has been invaded a total of eighty times during its recorded history.

Sparta ruled the island in the 6th century BC, and kept a close watch, annually sending a governor, as it was on the trade routes to Egypt, Crete and Libya, as well as being an advance post for attacking pirates.

In 10 AD Arabian attacks from Crete caused the island to become deserted. The Venetians landed in 1204, but the Byzantine empire won it back, and when the Turks conquered the Peloponnese, many Byzantine noblemen sought refuge on Kithira. Marriage united the Byzantines and the Venetians but, as detailed, the Turkish pirate Barbarossa 'dropped in' during 1537.

The Venetians, who called the island Cerigo, returned in the 15th century and instituted the 'Golden Book'. This was also in use on other islands (Lefkas, for example) and was a 'family tree' system of recording nobility and serfs.

The Turks reconquered the island in the 18th century. The Venetians regained it, followed by the Turks, then the Venetians, and finally Napoleon showed up in 1797 and took Kithira for France, along with the other Ionian islands. The locals burnt the 'Golden Book' and marched along to the tune of the Marseillaise and, apart from a brief period of Russo-Turkish suzerainty, it remained under French rule until it was handed over to the British, in 1814. The latter stayed in control for fifty years: as local sources put it, "Although it was clear that the British had no-one's interests at heart, but their own, they continued to employ the excuse of the need for protection"! In 1864 Kithira was finally reunited with the rest of Greece.

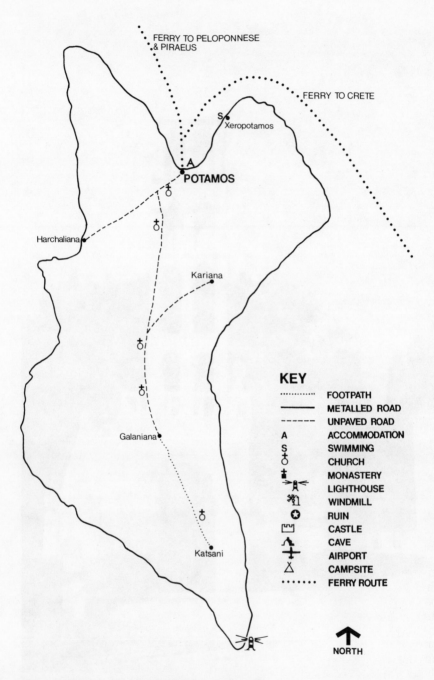

FERRY TO PELOPONNESE & PIRAEUS

FERRY TO CRETE

S
Xeropotamos

A
POTAMOS

Harchaliana

Kariana

Galaniana

Katsani

KEY

··········	FOOTPATH
——	METALLED ROAD
– – –	UNPAVED ROAD
A	ACCOMMODATION
S	SWIMMING
⚲	CHURCH
⚲	MONASTERY
	LIGHTHOUSE
	WINDMILL
⊛	RUIN
⌷	CASTLE
⋀	CAVE
	AIRPORT
⋀	CAMPSITE
• • • •	FERRY ROUTE

↑
NORTH

Illustration 16 Antikithira island

On a scale of 1 to 5:	Sites to visit: 1
Appeal: 3	Accessibility: 1
Exploitation: 1	
Beaches: 1	
Scenic Beauty: 3	Alternative Names: Lioi('Lee')
Accommodation - standard: 2	Population: 100
Accommodation - availability: 1	Telephone prefix: 0735
Facilities: 1	Size: 10km long and 5km wide

Location
Between Kithira and Crete, south of the Peloponnesian mainland.

Getting There
Airport: No, but see Kithira.

Ferries: Antikithira is subject to adverse weather conditions, and Potamos port is poorly protected from the north winds. If it is blowing, the chances of getting on or off the island are slim.

The Car ferry 'Ionian' from Piraeus, via Neapolis, Githion and Kithira, calls twice weekly, returning in the opposite direction, a few hours later, from Crete (see Kithira island for the route description). There are no other scheduled ferries, but a weekly caique from Kapsali (Kithira) brings supplies, so hardy souls might be able to hitch a lift on that craft.

General
Antikithira's appeal is its remoteness. This isolated island, near the deepest part of the Mediterranean and surrounded by some of the roughest waters in Greece, is a rugged but fertile spot, with a close-knit community of farmers and fishermen. Most people live in Potamos, but the hamlet of Galaniana, in the south, has twenty-five residents.

The period between 1983 and 1988 was called the 'salvation years': electricity, running water, a doctor, a ferry boat quay and a road (to replace the footpath), appeared in quick succession. One hopes all the effort was not too late, because the island deserves to survive. With plentiful water (as yet unplundered by the excessive demands of tourists) and well cultivated land, the community is almost self-supporting, a unique claim on such a small island. The population produce fruit and vegetables, honey, a good local wine, and its grassy slopes feed more goats than are needed for their own use. Petrol for tractors and caiques is the only important commodity which must be shipped in from Kithira, on a weekly basis.

Incidentally, information about Antikithira can sometimes be obtained from the large, villa-style building on the main promenade at Kapsali, Kithira. This is opposite the beach and has "Antikithira" written above the door. The hostel-like set-up, complete with beds and cooking facilities, is provided for Antikithirans, when 'visiting'. Island officials (*koinotita*), in particular the stern-looking but extremely helpful secretary of the island, are based here during their frequent visits to Kithira.

Accommodation
The island authorities have a plan to build rooms, in the near future, but at present only ten are available in private homes, which may or may not have piped water - currently being installed.

Camping There is no official site, but wild camping is not discouraged.

Food and Drink
A fair amount of food is home produced and there is a kafenion in Potamos, which serves some meals during the season. The *Koinotita* intends to provide a taverna, sometime in the future...

Vital Information
Well, there is a policeman, based at Potamos, and the other 'officials' include the priest and the lighthouse keeper. Electricity was installed in 1984, and as mentioned, running water is in the process of being 'put into' he pipes, right now. The village of Galaniana, further south, is not connected to the generating station, and employs solar-powered electricity.
There is a metered telephone in Potamos, and another in Galaniana. Potamos has one general store, and a village woman regularly bakes bread, in a wood-fired oven, for the whole island. There is no bank, no post office and no exchange office - bring your drachmae with you! The island does have a doctor, whose office in Potamos doubles as a pharmacy.

Beaches
Most of the coastline is steep and rocky. The island's only beach is at Xeropotamos, a short walk from the port.

Excursions
The only excursion is a two hour walk between Potamos and Galaniana, along the new track, which is now passable by car and agricultural vehicles.
Galaniana possesses a telephone and 'hosts' the monastery of Agios Miron, which celebrates its *yiorti* on August 17th. Beyond Galaniana, a mountain path leads to the hamlet of Katsani, which is almost deserted.

Island Customs, Feasts, Specialities and History
History The island is of volcanic origin, proof-positive being the number of sea shells and fossils that can be found embedded in hinterland rocks.
One of Antikithira's earliest names was 'Satyr', as its first inhabitant was thought to belong to that race, and to live in an island cave.
The first known human inhabitants apparently turned up in 2000 BC - a dozen robbers from Thessaly. Throughout ancient times, the inhabitants were a mixed bag of farmers and pirates. In 11 BC, seventy-four Cretan ships, returning from the Trojan war, were attacked by Antikithiran pirates. The ships escaped, but the enraged Cretans attacked the island to exact

revenge, raiding and burning everything. For the first time in its history, but not the last, Antikithira was bereft of any people.

New settlers from Crete and Monemvasia, in the Peloponnese, began to build towards the island's golden age, in the 3rd century BC. By then, Antikithira was a cultural centre, with a great harbour, trade ships, temples, a theatre and a reputable School of Philosophy, which produced the famous ancient philosopher, Straton. The town was known as Aigilia, and a few remains, including a city wall, are visible in the Potamos area.

The island was so wealthy that it even minted its own currency - a triangular silver coin with a small ring so it could be attached to a neck chain. The prosperity ended in the 1st century AD when the Romans swept through Greece, after which the island was abandoned once again, for two hundred years.

In 40 AD, forty-five Christian families, fleeing the Romans, landed and began the church building period. Future generations were not so holy, and piracy became more popular: in 482 AD a ship travelling from Venice to Crete, laden with gold, put in to port during a storm... and vanished. History repeated itself - angry Greeks dispatched soldiers to wreak revenge, and most of the islanders fled. Those who remained hid in a cave, but unfortunately their hiding place was discovered, and tradition holds that a great stone was placed over the entrance to the cavern - which was the end of those islanders. The stone is reportedly still visible, outside the cave, on the slopes of Mount Plagara. The island then remained deserted for a further two hundred and fifty years.

The fourth and last depopulation occurred during the Second World War when, in 1943, the Germans exiled all four hundred inhabitants to Crete, after reports that they had been helping English soldiers. The numbers have yet to recover - is the next depopulation just around the corner?

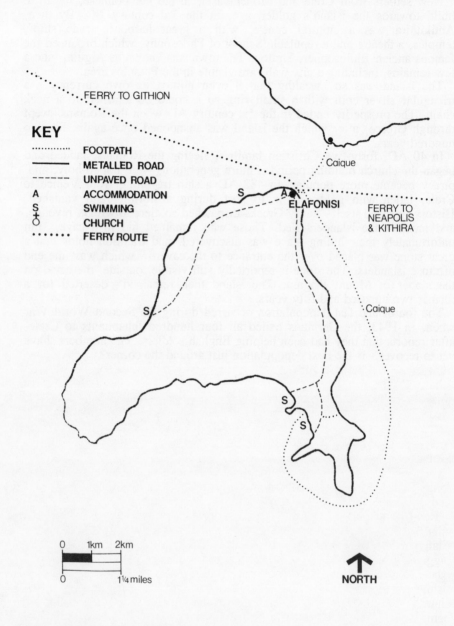

Illustration 17 Elafonisi island

CHAPTER TWELVE   ELAFONISI

On a scale of 1 to 5:	Sites to visit: 1
Appeal: 3	Accessibility: 2
Exploitation: 1	
Beaches: 5	Alternative Names: Elafonisos
Scenic Beauty: 3	Population: 500
Accommodation - standard: 2	Telephone prefix: 0732
Accommodation - availability: 2	Size: Approx. 4km from east to
Facilities: 2	west; 5km from north to south.

Location
A stone's throw from the south-east Peloponnesian mainland, the island is approximately 7km due west of the mainland port of Neapolis, and 9km due north of the tip of Kithira island.

Getting There
Airport: No but see Kithira.

Ferries: Elafonisi is awkward to reach, unless based in the village of Agonistis (sometimes called Biklafia) on the adjacent mainland, whence an hourly, summer-month caique shuttles back and forth to the island. Those who miss the boat can virtually swim across!

Connections with the capital are limited so few Athenians travel, simply to visit. In high season the Ionian calls in twice a week, on its convoluted route between Piraeus and Crete (see Kithira for details), but in peak season Elafonisi is linked daily with Neapolis port (Peloponnese) and Kithira island, by the FB Elafonisi. Before mid-July and after the end of August, this ship visits less frequently. There is also a local evening connection with Neapolis throughout the summer. Thus anyone touring the Peloponnese by car, or spending a holiday on Kithira, will easily be able to drop in.

General
Every visitor to Greece should visit a beach similar to that at Elafonisi. The long, clean, empty sands of **Simos** are unquestionably the island highlight, and are still completely undiscovered and undeveloped.

Remove the beach, and Elafonisi would be an ordinary, 'fishy' little island, with one pleasing, but unspectacular village. This is the port of Elafonisi, which imparts a lasting impression of dirt streets and higgledy-piggledy housing. A line of fish tavernas strings along the waterfront, where octopi hang out to dry on horizontal poles, above dozens of small fishing boats bobbing in the harbour. The picture is completed by the church of Agios Spiridon which appears shimmeringly to float on the sea, being situated at the end of a long causeway. The settlement is a lively place, if nothing special. But then there's the beach...

Accommodation
The limited accommodation on offer is located along the port waterfront, above the island's tavernas. A few more houses with rooms can be found to the far left of the harbour (sea behind one), in a pretty, residential area. There may not be enough space for visitors in peak season, although a lack of rooms, rather than hordes of tourists, is responsible for this situation.

Camping There is no official site, but those 'in the know' come to Elafonisi to camp at Simos beach (see Beaches).

Food and Drink
The seafront tavernas cater for the mainland Greeks, who stream over to Elafonisi at weekend lunchtimes, to eat fish, a favourite Greek pastime. These 'invasions' result in some temporary overcrowding. In among the traditional tavernas are a few, more modern, ice-cream and plastic-chair style cafes, but thankfully not very many.

Vital Information
Elafonisi doesn't have a bank, post office, OTE (a couple of the cafes have metered telephones), police or port police offices - the port policeman, who controls the harbour, comes over from Neapolis on the first ferry of the day. In 1975 a policeman was installed, but as he was never allocated an office, not surprisingly, he left, and has not been seen since... There are a couple of small supermarkets, bordering the main village street, which runs back from the seafront, almost opposite the small ferry boat quay, but quickly becoming a gravel track. Next door to the larger supermarket is a fresh water tap. There is a bakery and a doctor, both in the main village. Elafonisi hasn't a ferry boat ticket office, but timetables are displayed outside the Cafe To Gountagio, at the far end of the promenade, away from the chapel.
There is no moped hire, and no official public transport either, but fishing boats and a water taxi serve the beaches. This 'taxi' visits both beaches, which are on different sides of the island, twice a day in the summer months. If it is windy, the boatman is forced to go the long way round to reach Simos beach, which takes twice as long as the more usual route, but at least he can be relied upon to make the journey.

Beaches
I may have described a few of my discoveries in these pages as "...one of the best beaches in the Aegean". Well, Simos beach can only be challenged by one other beach I have ever seen (Porto Katsiki on Lefkas) for the title of the best beach in all of Greece. The track, which connects it with the town of Elafonisi, is very rough, even bare rock in places and it is about one hour's walk.
The outstanding feature is an islet of sand dunes in the bay which have joined to the beach by a wide bar of smooth sand. This effectively divides Simos into two great sweeping curves of white sand which stretch for miles. Even in August, there is hardly a soul in sight. The shallow seas and sandy

sea-bed result in bright turquoise waters. During July and August, a shack on the sandbar opens to sell (very necessary) bottled water, as well as some snacks and supplies, to the scattered campers, who take advantage of the few low trees beside the beach for shade. Camping sites do not come much more perfect than this.

The island has a second beach, **Panagia**, a half-hour walk along   the gravel road, which parallels the town beach of **Kondogomi**, on the opposite side of the island from Simos. This is long and sandy, and on any other island would be a star attraction, but it cannot compare with the unqualified, gratifying beauty of Simos.

Sites to See/Excursions
See Beaches.

INDEX

Pictures by: Anne Merewood/
Geoffrey O'Connell

GROC's Candid Guides to
THE GREEK ISLANDS

Other titles in this series.

published by Ashford, Buchanan & Enright
1 Church Road, Shedfield, Hants, England, SO3 2HW